VIRTUAL PEER REVIEW

VIRTUAL PEER REVIEW

Teaching and Learning about Writing in Online Environments

Lee-Ann Kastman Breuch

State University of New York Press

Published by
State University of New York Press, Albany

For information, address State University of New York Press,
90 State Street, Suite 700, Albany, NY 12207

Production by Diane Ganeles
Marketing by Susan Petrie

Library of Congress Cataloging-in-Publication Data

Breuch, Lee-Ann Kastman, 1970–
    Virtual peer review : teaching and learning about writing in online environments /
Lee-Ann Kastman Breuch.
        p. cm.
    Includes bibliographical references (p.) and index.
    ISBN 0-7914-6049-5 (alk. paper).
    1. English language—Rhetoric—Study and teaching—Data processing. 2. English
language—Composition and exercises—Computer-assisted instruction. 3. English
language—Composition and exercises—Data processing. 4. English
language—Rhetoric—Computer-assisted instruction. 5. Report writing—Study and
teaching—Data processing. 6. Report writing—Computer-assisted instruction. 7. Online
data processing. 8. Peer review. I. Title.

PE1404.B735 2004
808'.042'0285—dc22
                                                                    2003059025

10 9 8 7 6 5 4 3 2 1

For Peter

Contents

Acknowledgments

The beginning of my journey on this book can be traced back to a hike in the Alaskan wilderness outside of Juneau, where friends and I were on our way to a remote cabin. There, far away from computers, teaching, and my normal routine, I paused to consider that several computer-based writing practices revolved around the sequence of creating text, sending text to peers, and corresponding with peers about text. Considering this sequence, I recognized the activity in terms of peer review, and decided to further investigate connections between the sequence I identified and peer review scholarship. What I discovered is that computer technology has multiplied the accessibility and potential uses of peer review, not just for writing instruction, but also for workplace and daily writing activities. What I also discovered is that scholarship in writing studies, to this point, has not addressed virtual forms of peer review in any substantial way, nor have many scholars investigated the ways that computer technology may shape (for better or worse) the way peers respond to one another about writing.

I will forever be grateful for that moment of clarity in the Alaskan wilderness, as well as for the friends who accompanied me on that hike: Peter Breuch, Emily and Corey Wall, and Bryce and Amy Narveson. Thank you for listening to the kernels of my idea and discussing the potential directions that could result. Thanks also to colleagues who provided feedback on early versions and presentations about virtual peer review: Laura Gurak, Art Walzer, Pamela Flash, Lillian Bridwell-Bowles, Morgan Gresham, Hugh Burns, Rebecca Burnett, and Bernadette Longo. Special thanks to members of the ATTW research workshop during the spring 2002 conference; to Paul Anderson for directing me to CPR™ and Stuart Selber for recommending a "scenario approach" for illustrating virtual peer review; to the Monaco Group for support on the project. Many thanks to Steve Simmons and Mike White for their reflective feedback about technology and peer review in writing-intensive courses.

I am indebted to the College of Agricultural, Food, and Environmental Sciences at the University of Minnesota for granting me a single-semester leave to work on this project; and to University of Minnesota Grant-in-Aid of Artistry and Scholarship for awarding me with funds for research assistance. Special thanks to Jim Oliver for assisting me with so many tasks on this project—especially for providing insightful feedback and comments on early chapter drafts and for coding data in the case study. Thank you to Priscilla Ross, my editor at SUNY Press, for supporting this project and providing insight and generous assistance. Thanks as well to Diane Ganeles and Wyatt Benner for their thorough review of the book and assistance with its production.

A big thank-you to readers of my early drafts: Sam Racine, Mike Hassett, Kirstin Cronn-Mills, and Peter Breuch. Your comments helped me immensely and truly demonstrated the value of peer review! Thanks also to Andrea Breemer Frantz for your symbiotic support as we both worked on our book projects. Special thanks to my extended family that supported and participated in the project: Deb, Jim, Mike and Adam Moriarty, Ken, Diane, and Erik Kastman. Special thanks to Jim for his suggestions on the "Cousin Project" and to Ken for discussions about writing and interpretation at the Art Institute. Many thanks to participants of the "Cousin Project": Mike Moriarty, Erik Kastman, and Megan Hoover. A huge thank-you to Dr. Stanford Weisberg and Lexin Li, faculty and staff at the Statistical Clinic at the University of Minnesota, and to Dr. Andrea Olson for her expertise and advice as I worked through my case study. And finally, thank you to my family and friends, for unending patience and unwavering support as I worked on this project: Lee and Judy Kastman; Ruth Krohn; Scott, Lisa, Josh, and Sam Kastman; Tom, Carol, and Tyler Breuch; and Andi Olson and Mark Fellows. Thank you to Holly, for wonderful walks and for being my constant companion during long days at the computer. Finally, thank you to my husband, Peter, for your incredible support, patience, love, and for the thousands of ways you have helped me through this project.

Tables

Figures

Introduction

Although great strides have been made in the field of computers and writing, there is still a great deal of tension that surrounds the transition of writing instruction to computer-based environments. In *The Online Writing Classroom*, Susanmarie Harrington, Rebecca Rickly, and Michael Day explain that while computers and writing has successfully been recognized as a "subfield" of rhetoric and composition, some very practical problems impede any advancements the field has made. Problems may include lack of training among writing instructors to integrate computers into the classroom, and even lack of access to computer technologies for writing instruction (2).

In addition to these practical problems, I would argue that an even more fundamental problem exists, which is the resistance of some instructors to transition face-to-face instructional activities to virtual environments. For example, there seem to be equal amounts of enthusiasm and doubt about the usefulness of moving face-to-face activities online. On one hand, scholars have reported the successes their students have experienced using synchronous and asynchronous technologies to discuss writing—successes like increasing class participation and writing practice. On the other hand, some scholars have doubted the usefulness and relevance of moving face-to-face activities online, citing instances in which students merely played with technologies rather than engaged in meaningful discussions. Thus, although scholarship tells us a lot about computer-based writing instruction, the following questions remain: What do we gain by *fully* immersing our students in online learning environments, discussions and all? And what do we lose by making this transition?

In this book, I approach these questions through the lens of one of writing activity: peer review. Peer review is an instructional writing activity in which students read and provide commentary on one another's writing, and the purpose of this activity is to help students improve their writing and gain a sense of audience. In the past, peer review has been practiced face-to-face; for example, instructors frequently assign small group peer review workshops in class. In addition, scholarship about peer review celebrates social interaction that occurs specifically through oral communication. In fact, oral communication is the foundation for peer review as it is discussed in writing studies. That such a strong foundation in oral communication exists with regard to peer review makes the activity a prime candidate for examining the transition to online environments. Further, scholars have begun to reference peer review in online environments. As early as 1990, some scholars remarked that synchronous and asynchronous technologies would be quite suitable for activities like peer review (Barker and Kemp; Cyganowski). However, beyond mere mentions and an occasional reference, "virtual peer review" has received very little explicit attention in writing studies.

This lack of attention is curious, since the activity of virtual peer review—exchanging documents and feedback online for the purpose of improving writing—has become a common writing activity in both workplaces and academia. Virtual peer review has even been described as a *daily* writing activity. Yet we know very little about this common writing activity that relies not just on computers, but on Internet technology. Very seldom have researchers examined the roots of this activity in peer review theory and research; nor have researchers modeled ways to conduct virtual peer review. I argue we have much yet to learn about virtual peer review, specifically its potential instructional uses and the insights it may yield about face-to-face and online activities.

By focusing exclusively on virtual peer review, my close examination is simply one way to approach the larger questions about tensions that exist regarding face-to-face and online interaction. My hope is that through this examination we may glean insights that may better equip us to address transitions from face-to-face to virtual environments. We may learn, for example, how various issues and tensions converge and conflict, such as our commitment to sound composition pedagogy, our desire to learn more about computer technologies for composition, and our attitudes about using virtual, as opposed to face-to-face, environments.

In the case of peer review, I argue that the transition to virtual environments among classroom instructors is not as easy as it may seem. Deep-seated notions of peer review as an exercise of oral communication—rather than written communication—complicate such a transition, for virtual peer review reverses the primacy of oral over written communication so that written communication is king. Consequently, dialogue strategies that are typically employed for peer review change when placed online, and they are not as effective. Differences of time, space, and interaction impede our expectations of what can be accomplished in a "virtual peer review" session. In addition, despite the range of sophisticated technologies available to facilitate virtual peer review (specifically those that facilitate document exchange, online editing or commenting tools, and synchronous discussion), the reality may be that writers simply reach for the lowest common denominator to find what works across platforms rather than experiment with technologies that may not work across platforms. In the case of peer review, that lowest common denominator is e-mail, an asynchronous technology that can be accessed in several different ways. If instructors are unsatisfied with that lowest common denominator, they must be prepared to invest time introducing students to various technologies and helping them feel comfortable and confident in their potential uses.

These complexities run counter to an assumption I have often encountered—the assumption that the move of peer review to virtual environments is seamless. Some scholars have suggested, for example, that virtual peer review can be easily conducted outside of class or via distance and thus is more convenient for students (virtual peer review also saves valuable classroom time for the instructor). Certainly, conducting peer review online does introduce some conveniences, such as the ability to connect with reviewers across distance with great speed. Beyond these conveniences, I argue we all could use much more guidance *writing online*—particularly interacting through written communication (acknowledging the ways our interactive responses are influenced by differences of time and space), offering substantive critiques in writing, and taking control of various technologies to accomplish writing tasks. Virtual peer review is an activity that employs these goals, and as such it is an exercise in critical thinking as well as in technological literacy. In order to make this activity useful, I suggest we must be quite strategic in the ways that we write as well as in our choices and uses of technology.

The rest of this book, then, wrestles with the question of what happens when we take an activity that is grounded in face-to-face interactions and place it online. Does our understanding of peer review change when peer review is conducted in virtual environments? Is virtual peer review more beneficial to students than face-to-face peer review? What steps are necessary to implement virtual peer review in a writing classroom? What are the implications of this activity beyond the classroom? Can virtual peer review form the basis of an approach to teaching writing with computers?

To establish a pedagogical base for virtual peer review, in chapter 1 I review basic definitions of peer review and virtual peer review, and I suggest that virtual peer review is a kind of "remediation" that emphasizes differences rather than similarities between face-to-face and online interactions. I also situate virtual peer review within computer pedagogy scholarship in writing studies that emphasizes sound pedagogy and theoretical perspectives of technology.

To examine whether or not peer review changes when conducted in the virtual environment, in chapter 2 I suggest that as a remediation, virtual peer review has fundamental differences from peer review in terms of time, space, and interaction. For example, unlike face-to-face peer review, virtual peer review can suspend response time. Even synchronous discussions are somewhat suspended, and asynchronous discussions can lengthen peer review sessions so that they extend over several days. In terms of space, virtual peer reviewers may need to adjust to the lack of physical presence among their peers and learn to develop working relationships online. And, in terms of interaction, virtual peer reviewers must become quite adept at various forms of written communication, whether interaction, response, or formal evaluation.

In chapter 3, I discuss how differences in the virtual environment shape attitudes about peer review, and I argue that despite the growth of computer pedagogy, negative attitudes about technology still prevail. I explain this preference by suggesting that online discourse, while the subject of cutting-edge research in composition, can still be considered "abnormal discourse" in that it is perceived as an alternative to the "normal discourse" of face-to-face interactions in writing instruction. This is especially true in the case of peer review, which is grounded in oral communication and has for decades endorsed various face-to-face dialogic strategies. I argue that because virtual peer review involves full immersion in written communication, transitioning to this type of activity in the classroom may seem quite abnormal. Only a view of written communication as active accommodates this type of transition—I endorse in particular the view of "writing as involvement" as forwarded by Deborah Brandt.

In chapter 4, I discuss the challenges of implementing virtual peer review that relate to collaboration and technology. Specifically, I suggest that virtual peer review differs from face-to-face peer review in that finer distinctions must be made with regard to collaboration. For example, in addition to responding to writing, virtual peer review also can extend to collaborative activities of editing, collaborative writing, and collaborative thinking. The textual nature of virtual peer review, as well as the capabilities of technology to incorporate reviewer comments quickly and easily, raises issues of ownership and authorship that are not as urgent in face-to-face forms of peer review. In response, I suggest in chapter 4 that virtual peer review does not equal collaborative writing, for the goals of virtual peer review do not always include coauthoring a text. Virtual peer review also introduces challenges related to technology, such as selecting appropriate technology, dealing with the "frustration factor" or usability of a specific technology, and confronting negative attitudes about technology use. Each of these challenges can make virtual peer review more complex than face-to-face forms of the activity, contributing to the depiction of virtual peer review as "abnormal." I argue that if we are to begin embracing virtual peer review, we must acknowledge and address the challenges that emerge in the activity, always keeping in mind our goals for virtual peer review.

In chapter 5, I provide more guidance for the ways technology can be integrated in peer review. I advocate a goal-driven approach in which writers consider the goals they want to accomplish with their feedback and select technologies appropriate to those goals. For example, I review goals such as providing substantive, detailed feedback; providing summative endnote commentary; providing quick feedback addressed to specific queries; providing evaluation; and brainstorming. Each one of these goals may require a different type of technology; for instance, brainstorming may be best facilitated through synchronous technology, while substantive, detailed feedback may be best facilitated through asynchronous technology. The idea I forward in this chapter is that our goals for feedback must always drive our technological choices. Thus, I suggest that virtual peer review can be characterized in terms of "technological flexibility" in that it is not driven by one single technology but rather requires critical thinking about technology selection and use.

In chapter 6, I explore the implications of virtual peer review beyond the writing classroom. Specifically, I suggest that virtual peer review holds great promise for writing-intensive instruction across disciplines, online writing centers, and workplace settings. Virtual peer review allows for the integration of sound writing principles while encouraging the development of technological literacy.

I conclude the book by suggesting that virtual peer review offers a thorough, yet focused, look at computer pedagogy in composition today. Through the one lens of virtual peer review, we can learn about computer-based instruction, about attitudes toward technology, and about the promise of technology. In addition, this activity illustrates the potential of computers and writing well beyond the classroom, especially for workplace writing and electronic publishing. Indeed, I argue that because this writing activity is becoming so prevalent, we have a responsibility to study and begin to model this activity for our students.

Most of all, however, I wish to convey that virtual peer review is an in-depth example of how a common writing activity can be repurposed or remediated through computer technology. In the case of virtual peer review, writers must not only understand and appreciate social interaction, but be adept at using various writing technologies to produce and exchange feedback. Thus, virtual peer review encourages writers to take deliberate control of technologies and to think strategically, not just as writers, but as technology users.

CHAPTER 1

Virtual Peer Review as "Remediation"

It has been almost two decades since Kenneth Bruffee suggested in "Collaborative Learning and the 'Conversation of Mankind'" that peer review resembled the kinds of conversation that academics most value: social interaction between colleagues about scholarship (639). Bruffee described peer review as an activity in which "students learn to describe the organizational structure of a peer's paper, paraphrase it, and [suggest] what the author might do to improve the work" (637–38). Although peer review has long been practiced among writers (Gere), Bruffee shed new light on the activity, framing it in terms of social construction, a theoretical perspective characterized by the assertion that knowledge is created through social interaction. Specifically, Bruffee suggested that activities like peer review (and collaborative learning in general) highlighted the relationship between conversation and thought, while providing supportive environments for students to practice academic discourse. Indeed, Bruffee suggested that because peer review and collaborative activities resembled academic discourse, instructors had a responsibility to model this discourse for students. But the peer review that Bruffee described—peer review that scholars have documented and writing teachers have regularly practiced—tends to highlight social interaction in terms of oral communication; the role of writing in peer review is actually downplayed in this scholarship. For example, as several scholars have documented, peer review in classrooms typically occurs in the form of the face-to-face, in-class workshops between student pairs or student groups (Spear, *Sharing Writing*; Hawkins; DiPardo and Freedman; Gere), or more informally as sit-down discussions with other writers (Gere; Spigelman).

In this book, I suggest that a new form of peer review has emerged that is unaccounted for in peer review scholarship: a *virtual* kind of peer review. By "virtual" I do not mean "less than real" or "simulated," for this would suggest that virtual peer review is not a concrete activity. Rather, I refer to "virtual" in the computer sense; that is, activities that are facilitated by means of a computer. This new form of peer review is one that, unlike the peer review that Bruffee and others described, occurs without a single face-to-face discussion, because it is conducted in writing through computer technology. Specifically, through Internet technology writers can exchange documents through e-mail and attachments; they can communicate with one another about their work;

and they can edit or comment on writing using word-processing programs. This series of activities forms what I call "virtual peer review," or the use of computer technology to critique and to comment on another person's writing.

This new kind of peer review raises an important question for writing studies: to what extent does peer review change when it is entirely conducted through computer technology? The question is similar to one that Jay Bolter and Richard Grusin raise in terms of "remediation." Defining remediation as a "repurposing" of media, these authors argue that media shift and borrow from one another. They suggest that remediation is bound in a "double logic": it multiplies media while simultaneously seeking ways to erase it (5). To illustrate remediation, Bolter and Grusin use the examples of paintings being transformed to digital images, webcams imitating live presence, and the World Wide Web borrowing from print, yet transforming it. Bolter and Grusin suggest that remediation can happen in various degrees. For example, remediation can highlight older media in newer media; "refashion" older media entirely while still making the presence of older media apparent; emphasize stark differences between older and newer media; and absorb older media entirely, erasing their characteristics (47). They explain that a "repurposing as remediation is both what is 'unique to digital worlds' and what denies the possibility of that uniqueness" (50). Although Bolter and Grusin do not specifically address remediation in terms of face-to-face and electronic communication, I apply the concept in that way to examine the degree to which electronic communication "borrows" from face-to-face communication.

I am particularly interested in remediation as it applies to virtual peer review. Is virtual peer review a remediation of face-to-face peer review? Does virtual peer review borrow from face-to-face peer review, or is it its own distinct activity? The position I take is that while virtual peer review shares theoretical roots in peer review, virtual peer review has important, even fundamental, differences from peer review in practice. I therefore argue virtual peer review is a remediation of face-to-face peer review in the sense that it emphasizes stark differences rather than similarities. When conducted through computer technology, peer review emphasizes written communication over oral communication and shapes response in ways that reflect differences of time, space, and interaction in Internet environments. Thus, I suggest that peer response is shaped differently when conducted using computer technology. The consequence of this remediation, I argue, is that peer review has implications for writing studies beyond social theories of language that Bruffee and others have described. In addition to supporting social theories, virtual peer review also reinforces technological literacy in writing studies. I argue that we must investigate these differences more fully, especially as we integrate computer technology more frequently into our writing practices and classrooms.

However, I do not suggest that as a remediation virtual peer review erases or replaces peer review that is practiced in face-to-face environments. Rather, I suggest that the integration of computer technology into the activity *extends* our understanding of peer review as well as its pedagogical implications.

Throughout this book, I suggest that this remediation of peer review is not intuitive—that is, transferring peer review to virtual environments is not seamless. Difficulties in assimilating virtual peer review may arise in part because existing models of peer review highlight oral dialogue strategies and do not take into account the prominence of written communication in virtual peer review. For example, volumes of research have modeled face-to-face forms of peer review for applications such as peer conferences, collaboration, one-to-one tutoring, and teacher-student conferences (Harris, *Teaching One-to-One;* Reigstad and McAndrew; Flower et al.; Burnett, "Interactions"; Wallace; Spear, *Peer Response;* B. L. Clark; Gere and Stevens; Hawkins). No such guidance exists for virtual forms of peer review. As I suggest in chapter 4, moving peer review to virtual environments presents many challenges that require specific guidance regarding how to productively use computer technologies for peer review. We cannot expect that this activity is intuitive for writers. Therefore, in the spirit of Bruffee's call to model peer review for students, I argue we should consider modeling uses of *virtual* peer review.

This chapter begins, then, my exploration of virtual peer review. In the following sections I define what I am calling "virtual peer review;" provide background about the activity; and place it in the context of writing studies.

What is Virtual Peer Review?

Defining virtual peer review is difficult without first establishing what we mean by "peer review." Although I argue that virtual peer review differs fundamentally in practice from peer review, it is rooted in the same basic purpose as peer review: to respond to one another's writing. It is important to establish this basis for virtual peer review.

Defining "peer review" requires that we distinguish it from other group related activities, for peer review is frequently lumped together with a variety of activities to illustrate the broader appeal of collaborative learning. Anne DiPardo and Sarah Warshauer Freedman distinguish peer review by separating it from other collaborative activities, which they document in four categories: "responding to writing, thinking collaboratively, writing collaboratively, and editing student writing" (120). In considering peer review—also commonly referred to as peer response—they suggest that "responding to writing" is the most adequate category for the activity. In *Writing Groups,*

Anne Ruggles Gere also acknowledges the many ways peer review can be characterized, and she reaches a similar definition of peer review as "writers responding to one another's work":

> Writing groups, the partner method, helping circles, collaborative writing, response groups, team writing, writing laboratories, teacherless writing classes, group inquiry technique, the round table, class criticism, editing sessions, writing teams, workshops, peer tutoring, the socialized method, mutual improvement sessions, intensive peer review—the phenomenon has nearly as many names as people who employ it. The name, of course, matters less than what it described, which is writers responding to one another's work. (1)

Bruffee further specifies this definition, though he too acknowledges several possible names for the activity such as "peer criticism" or "peer evaluation" (637). He uses these terms interchangeably to describe an activity in which "students learn to describe the organizational structure of a peer's paper, paraphrase it, and comment both on what seems well done and what the author might do to improve the work" (637–38).

As these scholars suggest, peer review can be defined as *responding to one another's writing for the purpose of improving writing*. Gere points out that peer review has a long history, dating back to the early eighteenth century, in which writing groups were associated with literary societies of colleges and universities (10); peer review has subsequently been discussed in several contexts (Spear, *Sharing Writing;* Spear, *Peer Response;* B. L. Clark; Olson; Katz; Burnett, "Interactions"; Forman; Myers; Gross).

In contrast, virtual peer review has a very short history, and is only addressed sporadically in literature. Indeed, one of the frustrations in studying virtual peer review is that no concrete definition of the activity exists; as far as I can tell, even my use of the term "virtual peer review" is new. Certainly, several scholars have addressed *components* of virtual peer review, such as the influence of word-processing programs on revision (Bridwell; Wresch; Hawisher, "Effects"; Crafton) and the use of networked computers in the classroom (Cooper and Selfe; Hartman et al.; Bowen; Barker and Kemp). What is lacking in this literature is how these various aspects of computer technology can be pulled together to meet the specific purpose of peer review. In other words, few studies isolate the activity in order to extend our understandings and applications of *peer review* to include computer technology. Consequently, peer review scholarship must be revisited in order to accommodate virtual forms of peer review.

I define virtual peer review as *the activity of using computer technology to exchange and respond to one another's writing for the purpose of improving writing*. From this definition, one can see that virtual peer review shares the same basic task as peer review: responding to one another's writing. However, it differs in that computer technology must be used to interact with peer reviewers. Virtual peer review thus employs computer technology in three ways: (1) to write documents; (2) to exchange written documents electronically, using Internet attachments, networked computers, and word-processing; and (3) to converse with reviewers about those documents, through electronic comments produced either synchronously (real-time) or asynchronously (delayed time). This definition suggests that in virtual peer review, participants receive documents in virtual space, they read documents in virtual space, and they respond in virtual space. No aspect of this activity is conducted face-to-face. Virtual peer review thus shares the same task as peer review, although it is practiced differently using computer technology.

How Might We Be Familiar with Virtual Peer Review?

Given the background I have just provided, perhaps we can identify uses of virtual peer review in our own writing practices. I know this has certainly been true in my experience, particularly in publishing, but also for any document I might write. For example, I have come to rely on Internet technology to submit articles, chapter drafts, and presentation proposals, and I also use word-processing and e-mail in my own informal review processes when I send documents to willing readers, whether across the country or down the hall, to respond to my work. I rely on e-mail to receive comments from reviewers, and I frequently correspond with reviewers, editors, and presses via e-mail about ways to further revise manuscripts. For me professionally, the activity of peer review quite often is conducted entirely online. Thus, I have come to rely on computer technologies first to write, then to exchange my writing, and finally to correspond with peers. In addition, this practice is one that, when I think about it, I repeat for most writing projects.

In fact, chances are that most of us have experienced some kind of virtual peer review before—perhaps in the form of an asynchronous e-mail exchange addressing an author's writing, or perhaps in the form of the synchronous chat in which participants discuss ways to strengthen one's writing. Consider the following examples (all of which are *real*):

• A student group is writing a test plan for a usability project that is due in their technical communication class. But they have a crucial question about the test plan that they need to discuss directly with the client of the usability project. Because time is short, they will be unable to meet with their client in person. Using Web-based tools that have been provided for them, they decide to set up a synchronous chat with their client to discuss the test plan. They prepare for the chat by sending an e-mail to the client with their test plan attached.

- An online tutor receives an e-mail from a student desperately seeking help with a writing assignment. The assignment is due in a day, but the student will not be able to stop by the writing center for an appointment. The tutor suggests that they meet in the chat room of their online writing center at 7 p.m. that night. The two meet online to discuss problems the student is having with his paper.

- A marketer's job involves editing client publications on a daily basis. Specifically, he must generate text for items such as brochures and booklets, and he must also receive feedback on that text from several people. To manage this process, he writes documents using word processing, e-mails these documents to readers, and then asks readers to make comments using the "track changes" feature found within many word-processing programs. This feature allows him to see not only the changes his clients want, but it also assigns a color to each reader so that he can see who made what changes.

- A manager wants to update his resumé for an upcoming job interview. He knows a friend in another city would be willing to provide feedback, but he has very little time to make changes. He sends his resumé via e-mail as a word document attachment to his friend. In the text of his e-mail message, he writes: "Do you see any errors in my resume? Could you please send feedback by tomorrow at 8 a.m.?" He attaches his resumé, which is a word document, to the e-mail message and waits for a response.

- A freelance writer is submitting a story to a newsletter, but before she sends it she decides to ask her daughter, a professional writer, for feedback. She pastes the entire story into the text of an e-mail message, and asks her daughter for feedback on specific passages. Her daughter receives the e-mail and hits "reply." In the text of the message, she inserts line spaces and types her comments in ALL CAPS to distinguish her comments from her mother's original text. She then sends her comments back to her mother via e-mail.

These examples demonstrate that virtual peer review has begun to appear in classrooms, online writing centers, workplaces, and even daily lives. The fact of the matter is that virtual peer review is already here. Several other writing practices may already include virtual peer review; it is just that we have not *recognized* it in any consistent or formal way.

Instead, various terms such as "online editing" and "electronic collaboration" may have been used to describe virtual peer review in settings such as academic publishing, journalism, marketing, and technical communication. For example, in "Online Editing, Mark-up Models, and the Workplace Lives of Editors and Writers," David Farkas and Steven Poltrock cite advantages of "online editing" such as speed of editing process, efficient archiving, and integration in overall technology systems (160–61). They describe approaches to marking text online such as "the comment model" and the "edit trace model," which are intertextual comments that are inserted electronically. These authors note that online editing is sure to become more common, but that we must closely investigate technologies to find the best fit with editing practices (174).

In another account, online editing is discussed as a way to enforce peer reviews for submissions to an academic journal. In "Professional Counseling Journals: Implementing Online Editing and Peer Review," authors from an editorial board of the journal *Counselor Education and Supervision* describe a trial period established to test online review of journal submissions. They describe steps of this trial such as (1) the process of making submissions accessible in an online form; (2) making online review worksheets accessible to reviewers; (3) suggesting comment techniques; and (4) creating a Web-facilitated interface to direct the return of reviewers' comments. They cite a number of advantages of online peer review, such as a significant reduction of mailing costs, reduction of overall publication time period (from about two years to eight months), and reduction of copy costs (3). They describe the following process for conducting peer review online:

> Reviewers will also have the option of writing comments directly on the manuscript that they have opened in their word processors. Reviewers will be asked to write all comments with their word processors in a bold, uppercase font, inserted into the proper place in the file. The manuscript can then be returned to the Editor as an e-mail attachment in rich text format, or by fax. ("Professional Counseling Journals" 5)

Virtual peer review has also appeared in terms of electronic collaboration. For example, in workplace settings, Internets and Intranets have the power to connect employees, and they can easily facilitate the exchange of documents. When group members provide online comments directed at revision and editing, they are conducting virtual peer review within their groups. Yet as Janis Forman suggests, these collaborative practices introduce a number of complexities, such as different levels of technological familiarity among group members, identification and resolution of conflict online, and management of interaction dynamics in online environments (140; see also Burnett and Clark).

Although several scholars have articulated connections between collaboration and computer technology, virtual peer review itself is seldom highlighted in scholarship about electronic collaboration. Instead, as collections such as *Electronic Collaborators* (Bonk and King) and *Collaborative Virtual Environments* (Churchill et al.) demonstrate, scholars are interested in describing the *range* of collaborative technologies that can be employed by groups and the various impacts such technologies may have on group work. Thus, careful distinctions must be made between collaborative writing and virtual peer review. Recall that DiPardo and Freedman outlined differences between peer review and other collaborative activities; the same care must be taken when examining virtual peer review. Collaborative writing involves *coauthorship,* and technologies can facilitate the generation of text from multiple authors quite well. However, virtual peer review is not the same as coauthorship. Rather, feedback and interaction from peers in virtual peer review is directed toward the purpose of providing responses and suggestions to an author, not for contributing text that will be assimilated into an author's draft. Thus, it could be said that electronic collaborative writing includes virtual peer review, but not that virtual peer review always includes collaborative writing. Virtual peer review can be placed in the context of electronic collaboration only when given this careful distinction. Because this distinction is so important to virtual peer review, I revisit it in more detail in chapter 4.

One other place we may have encountered virtual peer review is online writing centers (also known as "Online Writing Labs" or OWLs), which are academic tutoring services designed to support student writers. In the past decade, several writing center scholars have explored ways that technology might be applied in tutorials, although most online writing centers exist in conjunction with a face-to-face writing center. Sources such as *Wiring the Writing Center* (Hobsen) and *Taking Flight with OWLs* (Inman and Sewell) describe innovations such as asynchronous tutoring sessions in which tutors interact with students through e-mail (Mabrito, "E-mail"; Castner; Monroe; Coogan, "Email"; Rickly). For example, Rebecca Rickly describes in detail how tutors can comment on student writing online in e-mail chats by distinguishing online peer reviewer comments through different symbols, fonts, colors, or styles on screen (Hobsen, *Wiring the Writing Center*). In addition, in "The Look and Feel of the OWL Conference," Barbara Monroe describes how tutors can comment on student writing by using a three-part structure in e-mail messages: front notes, intertextual notes, and endnotes. She suggests that through this structure, tutors can attempt to simulate interaction with students that typically occurs in face-to-face tutoring sessions. Asynchronous tutoring can be taken even further, such as in centers that exist completely online rather than as a supplement to face-to-face writing centers. Such is the case with the Online Writing Center (OWC), which I have both studied and administered at the University of Minnesota (http://www.umn.edu). Because this center exists only online, it defies the traditional notion of a writing center. For example, the OWC doesn't have a front desk for administrative staff, it doesn't have a physical library of sources (its sources are online), and it doesn't have rows of tutoring carrels. The OWC also doesn't have, as Muriel Harris has described, coffeepots or candy dishes to welcome tutees ("Using Computers" 7). In short, the Online Writing Center looks nothing like a traditional writing center, because its service and interaction with students exist in a virtual space. Instead, tutoring occurs asynchronously through a Web-based interface in which tutors can upload student's papers and comment using the structure Monroe described. (See figure 1.)

Virtual peer review is also reflected in accounts of synchronous tutoring in writing centers, in which tutors and students meet in chat rooms to "discuss" the students' writing. Eric Crump describes such a session as it

Attach File:
Browse...
Word processor:
Word for Windows (*.doc)
Computer: O PC O Mac O Unix
Date you would like your feedback returned:
(Please allow for a 72 hour turn around)
04-Apr-02
Type of document:
Choose one
Trouble Areas:
Click here for an explanation of the trouble areas [Select up to 3 categories by using Ctrl + select(PC) or Command + select(Mac)]
Content/ideas
Audience
Purpose
Development
Organization
Expression

Figure 1. Submitting Writing for Tutorial Review through the Online Writing Center

occurs in a MUD (Multiuser Dimension). He argues that synchronous technologies like MUDs are advantageous for writing centers because they encourage students to practice written communication even as they interact with the tutor online (178). In addition, synchronous tutoring has the advantage of what he calls an "'oralish' nature" (178); that is, synchronous tutoring—though written—is closer to face-to-face dialogue than asynchronous tutoring through e-mail.

As these account demonstrate, the activity of virtual peer review has begun to permeate several writing practices. However, while scholars have discussed what appears to be virtual peer review, they have done so in numerous contexts, using a variety of terms to describe the activity. A primary purpose of this book is to begin talking about virtual peer review by placing it in the context of peer review scholarship, which is based mostly on the field of writing studies—a field that emphasizes theory and pedagogy of writing. There are important reasons why I believe this context is appropriate for investigating virtual peer review. First, peer review literature up to this point does not often emphasize writing or computer technology in the activity of peer review; thus, an important gap in literature exists. Second, because virtual peer review is beginning to occur more frequently, we must begin learning more about this activity so that we can better model it for students or anyone else interested in learning about the activity. Third, extending our understanding of peer review to virtual environments may particularly benefit writing studies because of recent interest in computer-based writing instruction—a growing field in writing studies. In the next section I place virtual peer review more firmly in the context of peer review and writing studies.

What Do We Know about Virtual Peer Review in Writing Studies?

Surprisingly, virtual peer review has appeared only haphazardly in writing studies and has not been discussed in any substantial way. For example, some scholars have alluded to virtual peer review by suggesting it is the same activity as face-to-face peer review, except that it is conducted outside of class (Palmquist et al. 147–48; Palmquist and Zimmerman 39; LeBlanc 34; Berge and Collins 4; Ewald 130). Most of these accounts merely emphasize the convenience of virtual peer review and do not go into any detail about how to conduct the activity; the assumption underlying these accounts is that peer review does not change when introduced to virtual environments.

Brief descriptions of virtual peer review have also appeared in writing textbooks that emphasize the computer. For example, in *Writing with the Macintosh: Using Microsoft Word,* Ann Hill Duin and Kathleen S. Gorak describe how to use the computer to assess one's own writing. They provide a checklist and suggest opening two Word files on a computer—one with a formal text and one with a checklist—and using the checklist while scrolling through the paper (196). They suggest that this activity can serve to solicit peer feedback through e-mail (200). Similarly, in *Writing with a Computer,* Mike Palmquist and Donald Zimmerman suggest "reviewing and revising documents written by others" (39). They strongly recommend developing some kind of strategy for making comments online, which includes: "read first—correct later . . . highlight key passages and use the gist and predict strategies . . . create a document summary to identify key points . . . role play the audience" (40–41).

Indeed, the subfield of computer pedagogy within composition is where virtual peer review is most likely to surface, if it surfaces at all. However, the few accounts of virtual peer review that exist in this literature tend to be buried in larger discussions in support of using computers to teach writing (seldom is the term "peer review" used to describe the activity); thus, they are quite inaccessible. For example, Carol Klimick Cyganowski advocates the use of a computer lab environment for student groups. Although peer review is not the focus of her argument (rather she is arguing that computer labs are compatible with collaborative approaches), she asserts that "peer suggestions" (70) can be recorded using word-processing software. She remarks,

> The computer keyboard and disk storage seem to me a far more natural means of capturing peer collaboration and connecting to the writing process—a way for students to record their interactions, as well as a way to make those interactions and record an integral part of their inventing, drafting, and revising process. In the computer classroom, students' talking about writing and group writing becomes linked to keyboarding—trying peer suggestions and responding to alternatives immediately, using word-processing functions to invent, rearrange, and reinvent without disturbing the original text file. Students see interacting at and with the keyboard as more a privilege than a burden. (71)

In a discussion about the value of computers for interactive discussion in the classroom, Kathleen Skubikowski and John Elder also mention virtual peer review, but use the word "corresponding" to describe it (92). "After the students wrote for five days, they deposited their week's entries from disks onto the Appleshare network. Then each student would call up the week's writing of two assigned classmates, read it through, and respond to it both with interlinear comments and by writing a letter at the end of the file" (92). Thomas Barker and Fred Kemp describe virtual peer review but do so in the context of what they call "network theory." They suggest that networked computers benefit student writers: "Networked instructional systems generate many times more student-to-student transactions than traditional instruction, even when such traditional instruction is augmented by peer critiquing and group work" (17). To illustrate network theory, they describe how "peer critiquing" may occur in networked computer labs:

> If an essay is to be read and critiqued, then electronic mail is the means by which the critiques are transmitted and responded to. The way this usually works in practice is that a student enters the mail program and asks to see a particular document stored in the document database. This document appears in the upper half of the computer screen and can be scrolled up and down, beginning to end. The student then asks to send a mail message to the author of the document. An editing box, or scratch pad, appears in the lower half of the screen. The student reads the document in the upper half of the screen while entering comments in the bottom half. When she has finished commenting, she sends the bottom half off to the network as a mail message. When the writer of the formal text enters the mail program, he sees that he has mail, calls up the message, and if he wishes, responds to the message using the same split-screen technique that was used to critique his essay. (19)

Such contextualized accounts of virtual peer review appear sporadically. These accounts illustrate that virtual peer review has been both discussed and practiced in computer lab instructional environments; as such, they mark the beginning of scholarly discussion about virtual peer review in writing studies. However, beyond these brief mentions, virtual peer review has not been highlighted in any substantial way in this scholarship, nor has it been addressed using any consistent vocabulary. More explicit connections to peer review theory and practice are clearly necessary to further explore the ramifications of virtual peer review.

There are a handful of studies that do explicitly address virtual forms of peer review in comparison to face-to-face forms of peer review. In "Electronic Mail as a Vehicle for Peer Response," Mark Mabrito compared peer review responses between a face-to-face peer review group and an electronic peer review group. He analyzed the discussions of students in both groups; that is, he examined transcripts of spoken discourse from face-to-face groups and e-mail transcripts from electronic groups. He also analyzed differences in terms of "high apprehensive" and "low apprehensive" writers. Through his analysis, he found that "high apprehensive" writers participated more frequently in electronic peer review groups and offered more directive comments than they did in face-to-face groups. He also found that these students incorporated more e-mail peer review comments in their final revisions than they did in other kinds of peer review comments.

Similarly, in "Characteristics of Interactive Oral and Computer-mediated Peer Group Talk and Its Influence on Revision," Beth Hewett compared virtual peer review to face-to-face peer review (both synchronous and asynchronous). Hewett explored how peer talk functions in oral and computer-mediated peer review; she endorses the view that peer review is best when it involves a high degree of interaction. The results of her study show that students maintained interaction in virtual peer review but that "The talk itself had different qualities when students used different media, suggesting that the medium shapes the talk." She explains:

> With oral talk, gestures and body language supply cues that signal the particular receiver of the exchange, while they keep the talk open to the group as a whole. Including the entire group as interlocutors in the talk encourages interaction, which may lead to more intertextual idea exchanges. However, such intertextual sharing is complicated by CMC's [Computer-Mediated Communication's] hybrid nature. Lacking face-to-face cues, students must address their comments directly to particular peers, thus providing the appropriate context for reading them. Direct address to an individual, despite the fact that comments are posted to a common discussion list, lends the posted comments a mixed character as both public to the group and private to the individual. (282)

Like Mabrito, Hewett found that students were more likely to integrate peer comments into their final revisions; however, she attributes it to the fact that comments written in computer-mediated environments are interpreted by students as direct suggestions rather than idea sharing, an activity that is more likely to occur in face-to-face peer review.

More studies like these that explicitly address virtual forms of peer review are needed as we continue to integrate this activity into our writing classrooms, for they are beginning to show that there are differences between virtual peer review and face-to-face peer review. Overall, these studies have only begun to scratch the surface of understanding virtual forms of peer review; we have much more to learn about how different technologies may shape the activity, how writers can prepare for the activity, and whether or not virtual peer review significantly shapes the quality of response peers may offer each other.

In this book, I push this discussion further. I am particularly interested in the tension inherent in the issue of remediation. On the one hand, there is a desire to ground virtual peer review in the tradition of peer review as we know it and have practiced it (which is to say, within orality); yet, there is the reality that, as Hewett discovered, "the medium is the message" and that computer-mediated communication shapes peer review differently. In this book I seek to more fully describe virtual peer review by examining its roots in peer review but identifying its unique characteristics and uses. By working through these tensions, I seek to further explore the comparison of virtual and face-to-face peer review and discuss the implications of virtual peer review for writing studies.

Some may wonder if such an investigation is worth the effort; after all, if virtual peer review is different from peer review, what do we gain? By investigating this activity more closely, I argue that we gain a more concrete understanding of how to *take control of computer technology* in our writing activities, especially in terms of revising our writing. For example, we stand to gain a clearer understanding of the capabilities and limitations of synchronous and asynchronous tools for virtual peer review; rather than expecting these tools to simply imitate face-to-face discussion, we can better understand how to better use these tools for our benefit. In addition, investigating virtual peer review may provide important insights about computer-based writing instruction. That is, just as peer review has become a staple activity in writing classrooms as a way to reinforce process approaches, virtual peer review has the potential to become a staple activity in computer-based classrooms as a way to integrate computers into writing instruction.

Yet we know very little about how this "remediation" might take place. In the remainder of this chapter, I begin situating virtual peer review more fully in writing studies—particularly within computer pedagogy. Doing so requires an explanation of central issues in computer-based writing instruction, as well as an explanation of how virtual peer review relates to these issues. In the following sections I suggest that virtual peer review can be situated in computer pedagogy in the following ways: (1) virtual peer review actualizes the guideline that *pedagogy must drive technology;* (2) virtual peer review offers a lens through which to examine attitudes about face-to-face and virtual instruction; and (3) virtual peer review exemplifies issues related to technology uses and choices. All are issues that are present in writing studies today.

Virtual Peer Review Actualizes the Guideline
Pedagogy Must Drive Technology

One way virtual peer review relates to writing instruction—computer-based instruction in particular—is that it thoroughly responds to the guideline that *pedagogy must drive technology.* Because this guideline has become a mantra of sorts, further explanation is required to demonstrate the importance it plays in computer-based writing instruction.

The guideline *pedagogy must drive technology* can be traced back to Cynthia Selfe's 1989 book *Creating a Computer-Supported Writing Facility: A Blueprint for Action,* which provides excellent introductory guidance for teaching with computers (Kemp 268). The first two suggestions that Selfe offers in this book are the following:

SUGGESTION #1: Plan computer supported writing labs/classrooms so that they are tailored to writers, writing teachers, and writing programs, not computers.

SUGGESTION #2: Ground daily lab or classroom operations and instruction in the best of current writing theory, research, and pedagogy. (Selfe, *Creating* xx–xxi)

While these suggestions may seem rather obvious, Selfe explains their necessity: "In the rush to buy new equipment, to purchase new software, to establish a modicum of computer literacy among faculty members, we have not often had time as professionals to take care in the planning of computer use and computer facilities to support English composition programs" (22).

The idea bears repeating, for it is exactly right: it is easy to get caught up in technology, even to the point that we forget our immediate pedagogical goals. In a study about technology, distance, and collaboration, Linda Myers-Breslin reports that we *still* too often fail to put pedagogy first, concluding that "the initial challenge for teachers is to form a clear pedagogy and to focus pedagogical efforts" (167). Myers-Breslin suggests that technological bells and whistles continue to be a temptation, and that "far too often the technology drives our pedagogy. We must stop this trend. Our pedagogy must drive our technology. Only then can technology be used in productive (instead of merely intriguing) ways" (167). Thus, the idea that pedagogy must drive technology is not only common sense but is a necessary reminder for teachers (Harrington, Rickly, and Day 5; Kemp 269; Hawisher, "Blinding Insights" 54; Galin and Latchaw 45).

However, there is both wisdom and danger in the guideline that *pedagogy must drive technology*. The wisdom, of course, is that uses of technology will not be meaningful if we fail to consider the larger pedagogical goals we would like to accomplish. However, the guideline does not suggest any core of objectives that computers and writing should address. Therefore, the danger is that the guideline may give license to practically any kind of assignment, exercise, or course design. And it does. Composition scholars have reported an array of assignments and activities that can be employed in the name of *pedagogy must drive technology*, such as freewriting, brainstorming, conducting research on the Internet, keeping e-journals, publishing on the Web, and corresponding with pen pals. Scholars have also introduced programs to facilitate writing instruction such as Daedalus, CommonSpace, Groupware, ConnectWeb, writer's workbench, UNITE, ELIZA, MOOs and MUDs, e-mail, and more. Such variety demonstrates thoughtful and creative approaches to teaching writing with computers. Yet, as Susanmarie Harrington, Rebecca Rickly, and Michael Day point out in *The Online Writing Classroom*, sometimes the sheer number of options for teaching writing with computers is overwhelming, leaving instructors wondering how to begin the transition to teaching with computers (3). Further, from these diverse examples, it is difficult to discern any kind of coherent approach to teaching writing with computers. As J. Rocky Colativo notes: "The most damning wrong turn of writing instructions foray into the computer age is the shocking absence of any sustained body of scholarship geared toward discussing the practical side of teaching with technology" (154–55). Similarly, Fred Kemp notes the absence of a central rationale when he states, "I have never seen a computer facility based on a previously shared understanding of what instructional goals it was to serve" (270). Even Gail E. Hawisher, Paul LeBlanc, Charles Moran, and Cynthia L. Selfe admit to the lack of consensus regarding computer pedagogy, noting also that composition and rhetoric has seldom reached consensus on any pedagogical approach (49; see also Harrington, Rickly, and Day 3).

Recognizing the ways diversity has been valued in computer pedagogy, I do not presume that integrating virtual peer review will replace all other computer activities or that it will solve the issue of consensus. However, virtual peer review can be situated well within computer pedagogy, for its pedagogical assumptions are rooted in the well-established activity of peer review, and thus it exemplifies, from the start, the guideline that *pedagogy must drive technology*. For example, the basic activity of peer review is one we associate first with writing pedagogy. As I mentioned, peer review has a long history in composition; furthermore, it supports important pedagogical assumptions such as (1) writing as a process; (2) writing as a social act; and (3) student-centered approaches. Virtual peer review—conducted through computer technology—supports these assumptions as well. Let me briefly explain this common basis of virtual peer review with peer review. My purpose in doing so is to suggest that virtual peer review fully actualizes the guideline that *pedagogy must drive technology*.

A first assumption important to both virtual peer review and peer review is that writing is a process. This assumption suggests that there are recurring steps, phases, or stages in the writing act (Flower and Hayes, "Identifying"; Flower and Hayes, "Cognitive Process"; North; D. Russell, "Activity"; Kent). The distinguishing characteristic of process is the depiction of writing as an *activity* instead of a product—a characterization of writing that has inspired some to argue that process resembles a "paradigm shift" in composition from product-based to process-based explanations of writing (Hairston; Young). For example, in "Paradigms and Problems," Richard Young explains that the current-traditional paradigm emphasizes writing as the written product—the academic paper—whereas the process paradigm emphasizes activities leading up to the written product. As Stephen North puts it, the process paradigm encourages instructors to think about improving writers as opposed to improving papers (438). Although process can be traced back to the early 1970s (particularly through the work of Janet Emig), process came into full strength in the 1980s and has remained dominant (Halasek 3). Consequently, process has had enormous impact on the ways writing has been taught. Instructors who espouse process pedagogy frequently require students to revise their papers; some instructors even adopt approaches such as portfolio grading in which students have the opportunity to make unlimited revisions to their work.

Because of its inherent connections to process, peer review has become a common and staple activity in writing classrooms. For instance, when we consider that the purpose of peer review is to help fellow writers improve writing, naturally the exercise of peer review implies that a writer will revise his or her work, integrating comments and suggestions from the reviewer. However, virtual peer review highlights the role of computer technology in the writing process more than traditional peer review does. To illustrate, note the references to invention, drafting, and revision that Carol Klimick Cyganowski makes as she describes virtual peer review: "The computer keyboard and disk storage seem to me a far more natural means of capturing peer collaboration and connecting to the *writing process*—a way for students to record their interactions, as well as a way to make those interactions and record an integral part of their *inventing, drafting, and revising process*" (71, italics mine).

A second assumption important to both peer review and virtual peer review is the assumption that writing is a social act. This assumption derives from the belief that knowledge is created through our social interactions with others (most scholars refer to this as social constructionism). What is meant by this belief is that knowledge results from language and not the other way around. Bruffee explains this perspective by suggesting that language and thought are inextricably connected: "[T]he view that conversation and thought are causally related assumes not that thought is an essential attribute of the human mind but that it is instead an artifact created by social interaction" ("Collaboration" 640). Bruffee has perhaps championed this perspective most strongly as it relates to peer review and other collaborative activities; specifically, he suggests that teachers should find every opportunity to have students converse with one another about their writing while participating in peer review, small group workshops, or peer tutoring. Such activities, he argues, "[provide] a social context in which students can experience and practice the kinds of conversation valued by college teachers" (642).

Several scholars have further explored the connection of peer review with social theories of language, especially those forwarded by Vygotsky and Bakhtin (DiPardo and Freedman; Gere; Bruffee, "Conversation"; Spigelman). In her account of peer review, Gere endorses theories of language that acknowledge social contexts—what she calls "social genesis for language" (81), and she specifically advocates Vygotskian theories of language, which explain language development as a dialectic between individuals and social contexts. Gere suggests that social theories of language development are extremely compatible with writing groups and activities like peer review (83). Candace Spigelman also suggests the compatibility of social theories of language with peer review when she asserts that "socially constructed knowledge is both the basis and goal of writing group theory" (19). Citing Bakhtin, Spigelman explains that utterances in writing groups invite continued response, reflection, and further dialogue (18).

Although Bruffee, Gere, and others have made the connection between social interaction and peer review, this connection has largely been illustrated in terms of face-to-face peer review—specifically through terms such as "talking" and "conversing." However, when applied to virtual peer review, different words are used to describe social interaction—terms such as "correspondence," "conferencing," and "networking" (Skubikowski and Elder 92; Barker and Kemp 17).

Because of the lack of research on virtual peer review, and the inconsistency of vocabulary used to describe the activity, explicit connections between virtual peer review and social theories of language are rare.[1] Many more scholars have articulated the connection between social theories of language and a *range* of computer-based activities such as conferencing and online discussion. For instance, Galin and Latchaw assert in the introduction to *The Dialogic Classroom* that "the computers and writing community generally privileges social construction of knowledge and, by extension, collaborative models of learning" (18). Skubikowski and Elder similarly suggest that using computers in writing classrooms helps students develop writing communities and a sense of audience, and that these advantages of computer environments "are fundamentally compatible with the social-constructionist [rhetoric]" (104). In addition, M. Diane Langston and Trent Batson suggest that ENFI, or electronic networks for interaction, are social rather than individual (151) (see also Flores; Barker and Kemp; Handa; Galin and Latchaw, "Voices"; Palloff and Pratt). As this scholarship suggests, the connection between computer technology and social theories of language can be easily made.

Finally, both virtual peer review and peer review affirm the pedagogical assumption of student-centered learning. The idea of student-centered learning suggests that students become active rather than passive learners. As David Johnson, Roger Johnson, and Karl Smith put it, this type of learning presents a new paradigm for teaching, one in which "students actively construct their own knowledge" (9). In reference to peer review, Karen Spear remarks: "Working collaboratively, students must define problems for themselves and critically explore solutions; in doing so they practice crucial skills in listening, talking, and reading; in generating ideas, generalizing, abstracting, debating; and above all in assessing their own performance" (*Sharing Writing* 6). Consequently, this approach changes the role of the instructor from an authority figure to a facilitator (5). Pedagogical approaches like writing workshops, long advocated by Peter Elbow and Donald Murray, illustrate this change in teaching (Elbow 76–77; Murray 103). Adopting such approaches, Rebecca Laney describes how teachers must "let go" of impulses to direct peer review workshops rather than let students conduct their own workshops (151). Kristi Kraemer describes the importance of this shift: "I began to switch my efforts from fixing my students' writing to fixing my own teaching. My first task was that of convincing my students that they could work independently to produce clear, coherent text, and that it would be worth their while to do so" (138).

Virtual peer review likewise supports student-centered approaches in the classroom because, like traditional peer review, workshops can be facilitated by students via computer technology and seldom involve teacher intervention. Skubikowski and Elder explain: "We found our own roles as teachers change, first to that of the coach and then to an even more democratized role as we became aware that our voices on the network were not readily distinguishable from the voices of student correspondents" (103). Indeed, student-centered approaches are associated not only with virtual peer review, but with computer pedagogy in general. Many enthusiasts of computer pedagogy suggest that integrating computers into the classroom means that the teacher's role of authority figure shifts to coach or guide (see also Langston and Batson 144; Cyganowski 70; Handa 170; Palloff and Pratt 20).

As this brief review demonstrates, virtual peer review supports the same pedagogical assumptions as peer review and has a firm grounding in writing studies. It is easy to see, then, how virtual peer review may exemplify the guideline that *pedagogy must drive technology*. Because virtual peer review has a solid base in writing pedagogy, the activity of virtual peer review begins with pedagogical goals already in mind—how to help students revise; how to incorporate a sense of audience and social interaction; how to help students become actively engaged in writing. Because virtual peer review has a solid pedagogical foundation in writing studies, it has potential to become a useful instructional activity in computer-based writing classrooms.

In addition, I suggest that virtual peer review responds well to the guideline *pedagogy must drive technology* because it can be integrated consistently into a writing course. That is, virtual peer review can be employed for more than one assignment or even *every* assignment in a course. Such regularity would provide some sense of coherence in the way computers are integrated into writing classes. In *Transitions,* Mike Palmquist, Kate Kiefer, James Hartvigsen, and Barbara Goodlew advocate a similar approach with regard to consistency. They report that through using the "DAILYs" assignment, students can freewrite in response to a prompt at the beginning of each class; then they share this writing with other students in the class. Such regularity gives students a sense of accomplishment; while they may be unfamiliar with certain writing technologies at the beginning of a semester, by the end of the course they may be comfortable using, at the very least, word processing. Instead of integrating wildly different assignments that use different computer programs, consistent freewriting or virtual peer review could provide a sense of coherence.

Virtual Peer Review Provides a Lens to
Examine Attitudes about Computer-Based Instruction

A second way virtual peer review relates to writing studies is that it illustrates the complex range of attitudes that exists among teachers who are hesitant to integrate computers into their classroom. In a sense, virtual peer review can be a "lens" for further examining both resistance to and support of computer pedagogy.

As many scholars have noted, teaching with computers presents several challenges. Brad Mehlenbacher notes that obstacles exist in almost every direction for instructors wishing to integrate computers into their classrooms: "When we choose to bring technology into the classroom, we run numerous risks and invite several potential problems. We draw on real-world problem sets that may or may not make much sense to our colleagues. We deviate from hand-held one-to-the-many assignments and we complicate the simple elegance of face-to-face exchanges over deadlines, worries, frustrations, and so on" (233–34). Ultimately, Mehlenbacher suggests that we embrace these challenges and "give our students learning environments that are energized, playful, and unpredictable—the stuff of learning" (234). However, not all instructors are as ambitious or hopeful. As Fred Kemp suggests, computer pedagogy faces a strange obstacle that he describes as "the Resistance" (capital *R*), which is comprised of faculty members who refuse to integrate computer technology into their teaching (268). Kemp explains that this rejection of computer pedagogy could stem from any number of factors, such as lack of experience with computers or frustrations about administrative mandates to use technology (270). But mostly, teaching with computers requires a significant change in teaching approaches, and many teachers are simply unwilling to make this change, especially those who have managed for years without computers in the classroom.

Recently, more scholars have argued that the time may have come to view computer pedagogy as a *responsibility* rather than a choice. For example, in *Literacy and Technology in the Twenty-First Century,* Cynthia Selfe asserts that "Literacy alone is no longer our business. Literacy and technology are. Or so they must become" (3). Selfe explicitly states that her purpose is "to convince teachers of English studies, composition, and language arts that we must turn our attention to technology and its general relationship to literacy education" (5). She passionately encourages writing instructors to become involved in literacy and technology on several levels: curriculum committees and assessment programs, professional organizations, scholarship and research, instruction of first-year and advanced composition courses, and computer facilities (149–54). She argues that "the price we pay for ignoring this situation is the clear and shameful recognition that we have failed students, failed as humanists, and failed to establish an ethical foundation for future educational efforts in this country" (5).

Selfe's call to action has been echoed by scholars in various ways, and seems to reflect increasing attention toward computer pedagogy in writing studies. For instance, some scholars have painfully pointed out that resistance to computer pedagogy is ironic when we consider that we may also be regularly using computer technologies in our own academic discourse in the most basic of ways: to write, to communicate with colleagues, to publish. As Joan Tornow suggests: "Writing teachers simply cannot afford to ignore the fact that writing is increasingly an activity that occurs online" (2). Hawisher, LeBlanc, Moran, and Selfe describe this recognition as "the Copernican turn," or the realization that the computer is not merely a device or database, but rather a writing instrument (46). They suggest that this turn has amounted to a paradigm shift within computers and writing (46). Yet, clearly, some have made this turn and others haven't. Why? Such a question cannot be answered simply. Citing "the romantic rejection of technology," Kemp explains that "the presumed sheer mechanics of computing threaten in many people's mind to reduce an art [teaching] to little more than a procedure" (272), and he further suggests that

> The struggle does not hinge on educating the senior personnel or demonstrating how well this or that works. . . . The issue is not functionality, but rather fears of transition, of loss, and of the unthinkable invalidation of the work of lifetimes, and so much of it occurs unconsciously, beneath a presumption that instructional effectiveness is the only issue on the table. (273)

Although these arguments acknowledge the complexity of transitioning from traditional to computer-based classrooms, the fact remains that these arguments do not excuse us from recognizing our own reliance on technology. As Kemp states: "Once those in English studies recognize that their principal activity, working with words, in this day and time is an activity clearly dependent on word processing, network information access, and electronic publishing, then computers and networks stop being glamorous and start becoming essential . . ." (280). Thus, even though a range of sensitive and complex attitudes about teaching writing with computers exists, scholars are more frequently suggesting that computers can no longer be ignored in writing instruction.

Virtual peer review displays a similar range of attitudes regarding virtual and face-to-face peer review practices. As I suggest in chapter 3, there appears to be a kind of "normal discourse" regarding peer review that consists of face-to-face, sit-down discussions, whereas virtual peer review at times seems to be regarded as "abnormal discourse." As Bruffee explains, citing Richard Rorty, normal discourse *maintains* knowledge created in a community, but abnormal discourse *generates* new knowledge within a community (qtd. in "Collaboration" 647). Rorty also suggests that abnormal discourse is commonly met with resistance; that is, abnormal discourse is rarely accepted by the community and is frequently dismissed. Traces of these categorizations exist when we examine virtual peer review. For example, dialogue strategies involving face-to-face interaction (like Rogers's nondirective approach) no longer apply to virtual environments; "human" connection appears to be lost in cyberspace; and the lack of social cues means less feedback for students. Many instructors say transitioning peer review to virtual environments may simply not be worth the effort (Peckham). Others have flatly rejected virtual forms of peer review, because they do not produce the same benefits as face-to-face interaction (Harris, "Using Computers"; Russell, "Clients"). These types of reactions are common among those who expect virtual environments to imitate face-to-face environments; the result, unfortunately, is the casting of virtual peer review as an "abnormal" approach that goes against the grain of well-established research about face-to-face interactions.

However, when we focus on benefits, we see that virtual peer review offers some concrete advantages. As some scholars suggest, one of the primary and perhaps obvious advantages of activities like virtual peer review is that students practice writing more often (Condon; Harris and Pemberton). A resulting advantage is that authors receive written comments they can archive and thus *remember* from their interactions with peers (Mabrito, "Electronic Mail"; Hewett). In addition, virtual peer review can help students improve their sense of audience and purpose, because they have a concrete idea of who their readers are. As Thomas Barker and Fred Kemp report: "As students grow aware of how they themselves respond to the words and phrases of their peers, they grow more aware of how their own words are being read" (24). Mike Palmquist also notes that activities like virtual peer review elevate the amount of student discussion in classes; he argues that online interactions transform classroom experience by encouraging student-centered and active learning (see also Skubikowski and Elder; Palloff and Pratt).

The range of attitudes about virtual peer review illustrates, on a small scale, the tensions we may experience when transitioning instruction to computer classrooms. As such, virtual peer review provides an interesting lens through which we can examine computer pedagogy as a whole. For example, just as virtual peer review may require a balancing act between pedagogical grounding and attitudes about computers, the same could be said about computer pedagogy. Again, one of the purposes of this book is to push this discussion further—in this case, to examine the ways pedagogy and attitudes about computers intersect, as well as the tensions that may result from this intersection.

Virtual Peer Review Exemplifies Issues Related to Technology

Finally, virtual peer review relates to writing studies because it is fertile ground for exploring both a range of technological tools and theoretical perspectives of technology; both are areas of interest to teachers and scholars of writing.

Virtual peer review offers some unique insights in terms of technological tools, because it is not tied to one specific technology or program. That is, virtual peer review involves a range of tools that can take several forms for the following basic tasks included in virtual peer review: (1) producing writing; (2) exchanging writing; and (3) conversing about writing. Table 1 outlines the range of options available for these activities. Because so many options exist, the activity is driven by pedagogical goals (rather than any particular program), and students can make a program work for them to accomplish those goals.

Table 1
Activities and Technologies Associated with Virtual Peer Review

Tasks	*Technology Options*
Producing writing	Word processing
Exchanging writing	File server/share ware
	Electronic mail
	World Wide Web
Conversing about writing	Software for inserting comments (ranges from word processing to specific programs like CommonSpace)
	Asynchronous discussions through electronic mail
	Synchronous discussions through chats, MOOs, MUDs

A similar range of technological options has been documented in terms of electronic collaboration. For example, Curtis Bonk and Kira King focus on "learner-centered technologies" in their book *Electronic Collaborators,* an edited collection of essays about computer technologies used for instructional purposes. They separate collaborative technologies into the following categories: "stand-alone system collaboration" (two people working at one computer terminal), "asynchronous electronic processing," and "multiconferencing: asynchronous and synchronous classrooms" (xxx–xxxii). Given the context that Bonk and King provide, virtual peer review demonstrates not just one of these categories but all three. That is, virtual peer review can be conducted asynchronously, synchronously, or even through stand-alone system collaboration. Thus, virtual peer review allows for a great deal of "technological flexibility"; in other words, virtual peer review can be conducted using any number of technological tools. In addition, depending on an institution's resources, tools for producing, exchanging, and conversing about writing can be accessed separately, or they may be integrated into Web-based courseware (such as WebCT or Blackboard). For example, an author may use word processing to write a document, open e-mail to attach the document and send a message to reviewer, and converse with reviewers using e-mail or chats. Or, using courseware such as WebCT and Blackboard, authors can access multiple tools such as chat rooms, e-mail, and archives from the same portal.

In addition to these technological choices, there exists a structured online program that was created for peer review in higher education—a program called Calibrated Peer Review™ (CPR). CPR, created by Orville Chapman and Michael Fiore at UCLA, was originally designed for instructors and students in the sciences, and it facilitates the exchange and rating of student writing. The authors of the program explain that they created the program to model the writing process that typically occurs among scientists (an argument similar to the one I made regarding Bruffee's model of academic discourse):

> CPR was developed on a science-based model. What do scientists do? Research begins with proposals. Scientists write research proposals and review peer proposals. Scientists do research and write and peer review research manuscripts. Peer review has a prominent role in the progress of science. Anonymous peer review is thus the model on which we built Calibrated Peer Review™. In the beginning, CPR was intended to serve large lecture sections in university courses in conjunction with the fully digital, Internet-delivered Molecular Science learning units. But in actual use, CPR has worked well at many levels, in varied courses and class sizes. (Chapman and Fiore [page 2])

The software for this program was developed in 1998 and is being tested and refined every year. That a program exists specifically for the activity of peer review strengthens, I believe, the argument I am making that virtual peer review may play a role in computer-based writing courses. Certainly, CPR is being used centrally as a way to reinforce writing in the sciences, as its Web site explains and as its 140 partner institutions can attest. CPR offers yet another option for implementing virtual peer review, not only in writing classes, but in science classes; thus, it adds even more technological flexibility for institutions considering the integration of virtual peer review into their writing classes.

In addition to accommodating a range of technological tools, virtual peer review demonstrates theoretical accounts of technology. Here I focus on the scholarship of David Bolter, of David Kaufer and Kathleen Carley, and of Christina Haas, for all of these scholars address the question of how computer technology influences writing. It is interesting to consider the theoretical ramifications of an activity like virtual peer review, which fosters reading, writing, and interacting online. In *Writing Space,* David Bolter suggests that one effect of electronic writing might be different interpretations of author and reader roles, interpretations created by the increased participation readers have with texts. Bolter argues, for example, that "Electronic writing emphasizes the impermanence and changeability of text, and it tends to reduce the distance between author and reader by turning the reader into an author" (3). In addition, Bolter suggests that electronic writing may influence the ways information is organized, particularly in regard to linear versus nonlinear structures. The overall argument Bolter advances in *Writing Space* is that technologies can fundamentally change our literacy practices. As he asserts: "[T]he very idea of writing . . . cannot be separated from the materials and techniques with which we write, and genres and styles of writing are as much determined by technology as [by] other factors" (239–40).

In terms of virtual peer review, Bolter's suggestion that author and reader roles converge in electronic writing is particularly insightful. Although Bolter uses hypertext to illustrate his point, asynchronous virtual peer review also illustrates how readers—peer reviewers—interact with text and become authors online as they comment on their peers' writing. As I show in chapter 5, when virtual peer reviewers insert electronic comments asynchronously, they create a new document that the author must then read and revise. As a result, virtual peer review may shift roles more dramatically than face-to-face peer review, in which reviewers do not interfere as directly with an author's text. Again, this shift in roles may be challenging and nonintuitive, particularly for peer tutors who are trained never to write on a student's paper. The converging roles of reader and writer raise interesting questions about virtual peer review.

In accentuating differences between face-to-face and virtual peer review, the work of Kaufer and Carley may be useful, because they advocate an examination of communication technologies in their own right rather than in comparison with orality. In *Communication at a Distance: The Influence of Print on Sociocultural Organization and Change,* Kaufer and Carley are interested in how writing technologies change communication for social and organizational groups. Within their inquiry, they identify "physical properties" of communication such as synchronicity, durability, fixity, reach, and multiplicity. By alluding to these physical properties, they suggest ways in which electronic communication may (1) make a communicative transaction more durable and "fixed" because it is in print form, and (2) facilitate delivery to many rather than a few people at a time, potentially increasing the "reach" and "multiplicity" of a message. In essence, they suggest that "communication technologies alter the physical properties of the communicative transaction and make the creation of artificial agents possible" (413).

Their description of texts as artificial agents is particularly relevant to virtual peer review. They suggest that "through texts, human agents can engage in one-to-many interactions with other agents without being physically present" (415). Thus, because of the advantages allowed by electronic communication, the use of artificial agents may be a motivation for communicating electronically at a distance. Kaufer and Carley assert: "[P]rint breaks the barriers of proximity and the geographic barriers to communication and social change" (415). Such a discussion contributes to the quest to explore face-to-face and electronic forms of communication, which Kaufer and Carley acknowledge (3). However, they suggest that oral and written communication not be put against one another: "We do not need to set up oral communication in direct conflict with writing, but rather to ask what new possibilities were opened up to speakers when they could also take advantage of writing?" (6).

Thus, Kaufer and Carley's approach to examining the influence of technology on writing can be characterized as one that seeks to identify properties of electronic communication so we can better understand how electronic communication functions in communities. Such a perspective is extremely useful for examining virtual peer review; thus, I embrace Kaufer and Carley's perspective wholeheartedly. I am interested in the new possibilities that virtual environments offer to the activity of peer review, and the properties identified by Kaufer and Carley offer concrete ways to describe characteristics of virtual peer review practice (which I identify more completely in later chapters).

Finally, it is interesting to consider how theoretical perspectives of technology may shed light on the context of virtual peer review—specifically, the instructional context that I have foregrounded here. Some of the contextual concerns that arise for writing classrooms may include funding, access, or technical support at educational institutions. Additional concerns may include unequal student access to computer technology, which may limit the potential of virtual peer review for writing courses. These concerns influence the technological choices we make as well as our uses of technology. Here we may gain insight from Christina Haas, who examines technology from a thoroughly contextual perspective by focusing on its history, its creation, and its uses. In *Writing Technologies: The Materiality of Literacy,* Haas reminds us that technology is not a separate entity (222). In making this argument, Haas counters what she calls "cultural myths" of technology: the myth that technology is transparent and the myth that technology is all powerful (35). On the one hand, the myth of transparency suggests that computers are merely tools or instruments that do not influence the writing act in any way. In response, Haas argues that writing itself is a technology and cannot be separated from technology (34). On the other hand, the myth of technology suggests that computer technology would influence writing in profound ways (35); in response, Haas argues this perspective is not useful, because computer technology subsumes human agency (35). She ultimately suggests that neither myth is useful for examining technology, because technology is more complex than either of these myths suggests; in other words, technology cannot be separated from context. Haas suggests that we always consider the contexts surrounding technology and that we not simplify our understanding of technology or its effects. In short, we must adopt a critical perspective on technology. Other scholars have highlighted similar issues, suggesting that as we consider technology for teaching, we must critically examine the contexts surrounding instructional technology, including the political landscape, funding issues, access to technology, and how social or cultural aspects influence the choices we make (Selber; Mehlenbacher; Haas; Selfe, *Technology and Literacy;* Warshauer).

As Haas and others remind us, computer technology is not merely an instrument; rather, it shapes and is shaped by the persons creating and using it. Keeping these arguments in mind, in chapter 4 I discuss challenges of virtual peer review that arise in context. I share an example of how students in two sections of a writing-intensive course used collaborative technologies to support various writing tasks. This particular case illustrates challenges such as the failure of designated computer technologies and resulting resistance to technology. In addition, the example demonstrates how easy it is to blur various collaborative activities when working in virtual environments. Through specific examples, I suggest that virtual peer review requires careful distinctions about collaboration as well as the technologies used to support collaboration.

Critical and contextual perspectives are also important to virtual peer review in terms of the tasks involved in virtual peer review. For example, one must carefully consider goals for providing feedback to an author and let those goals drive technological choices. In addition, virtual peer reviewers must think critically about the technological options they have for writing electronic feedback, considering whether or not their peer review partners will be able to access the technology they have chosen. The result of such critical thinking in virtual peer review is that it fosters a kind of technological literacy. Indeed, I argue that virtual peer review exemplifies technological literacy, for students must not only have familiarity with the technologies they have chosen, but they must also think strategically about their uses of technology for the activity.

Virtual Peer Review as Remediation

Having situated virtual peer review in the context of writing studies—particularly the subfield of computer pedagogy—in the remainder of this book I seek to define and describe virtual peer review more fully, arguing that virtual peer review has fundamental differences from peer review that has been documented in previous scholarship. In other words, I argue that the integration of technology into peer review has resulted in a remediation of the activity, changing the ways peers respond to one another about writing. In chapter 2, I begin describing the ways that computer technology changes peer review response in terms of time, space, and interaction; I explain these differences through research in computer-mediated communication, adopting Kaufer and Carley's terms of fixity, durability, synchronicity, and multiplicity. In chapter 3, I argue that one important consequence of these differences is that virtual peer review revives the role of writing in peer review, which has been traditionally downplayed in favor of face-to-face dialogue in peer review. Specifically, I suggest that virtual peer review presents an "abnormal discourse" of sorts that favors written communication over speech communication—a flip-flop of how peer review has been categorized by most scholars.

Given this background, in chapter 4 I discuss the challenges that arise as we move peer review to virtual environments—challenges related to collaboration and technology. Sharing concrete examples of virtual peer review sessions, I distinguish between forms of collaboration such as responding to writing, editing, collaborative writing, and collaborative thinking. I argue that, unlike face-to-face peer review, which mainly relates to responding to writing, virtual peer review can merge into categories of editing and collaborative writing, raising concerns related to ownership and authorship. Challenges related to technology also arise with virtual peer review, such as selecting appropriate technologies for the activity, the "frustration factor" of using technologies, and negative attitudes about technology. I suggest that challenges of collaboration and technology perpetuate the idea of virtual peer review as "abnormal discourse," especially since these specific challenges have not been addressed in peer review literature to this point. However, as "abnormal discourse," virtual peer review encourages us to think in new ways about peer review, acknowledge new challenges, and create new boundaries. If we are to expand our understanding of peer review to accommodate virtual forms of the activity, we must recognize challenges so that we can be better prepared to address them.

In chapter 5, I demonstrate several ways that virtual peer review may be enacted. I reinforce the notion that virtual peer review has great technological flexibility because it can be conducted using a range of technological tools. In addition, I illustrate how well-defined objectives for virtual peer review drive technological choices for the activity, actualizing a kind of technological literacy. In chapter 6, I discuss implications of virtual peer review for classroom contexts and beyond.

CHAPTER 2

Characteristics of Virtual Peer Review

As I mentioned in the last chapter, virtual peer review is not exactly a new activity. Rather, it has been described in literature in the following ways: (1) some scholars suggest virtual peer review is an intuitive activity that simply transfers face-to-face peer review to computers; (2) some scholars have described the activity but have labeled it differently; and (3) some scholars have alluded to the differences between virtual forms of peer review and those of face-to-face peer review. While these discussions of virtual peer review provide a healthy introduction, they do not sufficiently distinguish the new situations that arise when peer review is practiced in virtual environments. We are left knowing relatively little about the basic characteristics of virtual peer review or its primary differences from face-to-face forms of peer review—specifically, how computer technology changes the activity. Instead, we may bring to the table our *expectations* about how peer review might change when conducted in virtual environments and base judgments on those expectations. For example, countless times I have encountered the perception that "something is lost" when we take peer review online, as if the online environments were inferior in some way. People seem to want proof of the effectiveness of virtual environments. Questions I have frequently been asked include: Are virtual environments better than face-to-face? Are they cheaper? Are they more efficient? Do students learn more? Sometimes, the perception is that virtual environments are only worth looking at if we can prove that they are somehow better than face-to-face environments.

My response to these questions is always that such comparisons in terms of good/bad and better/worse do little good in exploring virtual environments for peer review. As Thomas Russell has argued repeatedly, studies have shown there is no significant difference in the effectiveness of instruction in face-to-face environments and those in online environments. He argues that it is fruitless to pursue the matter, hoping to find that one environment is better or worse. A much better approach, he argues, is to consider the differences of these environments and ask critical questions about those differences. And again, as Kaufer and Carley suggest, it is sometimes more productive to examine the *new possibilities* that arise when exploring online communication. Accordingly, my purpose here is not to suggest that virtual peer review is better than face-to-face peer review; nor is my purpose to suggest that we replace

37

face-to-face peer review with its virtual cousin. My purpose, rather, is to inquire about the differences so that we may begin to extend our understanding of peer review and appreciate what virtual environments have to offer.

In this chapter, I suggest that we might begin this discussion by looking at the basic ways computer technology shapes peer response—ways, I argue, that are different from face-to-face response. Although virtual peer review shares the same pedagogical assumptions as traditional peer review, the fact that it occurs in virtual environments means additional factors of time, space, and interaction suddenly become important. For example, when peer review is conducted virtually, time can become suspended—if conducted asynchronously, there is no longer the pressure of completing a peer review in a specified time period. In addition, computer technology allows peers to exchange writing with one another across distance, sometimes across the country, and sometimes across the globe. Further, virtual peer review facilitates a degree of interaction between peers through chats or messages, which is often less expensive than phone calls, letters, or interactive television. Certainly, the differences of time, space, and interaction suggest the potential of virtual peer review to be an extremely efficient, convenient, and inexpensive way to conduct the business of writing. In this chapter I do suggest, however, that differences must not be taken at face value. Writing scholars in particular must carefully examine both the advantages and disadvantages that computer technology affords peer review.

In the following pages, I begin outlining the ways virtual peer review changes in terms of time, space, and interaction. In addressing these characteristics, I review scholarship in the field of computer-mediated communication, which sheds light on issues of face-to-face and virtual environments for communication. In doing so I employ terms such as fixity, durability, synchronicity, and multiplicity that Kaufer and Carley use in describing features of electronic communication. In addition, to illustrate features of virtual peer review, I use examples from a case study of an animal science/agronomy course in which students conducted peer review in virtual environments (I explain the case study more fully in chapter 4). I conclude the chapter by summarizing distinguishing characteristics of virtual peer review.

Time

In terms of time, the difference of virtual peer review practice can be stated bluntly: traditional peer review occurs immediately, while virtual peer review is delayed. This difference requires more explanation regarding the technologies used for virtual peer review, and here I again note that virtual peer review as I am defining it does not rely on any one particular technology. Rather, virtual peer review can be conducted using synchronous technologies (such as chats, MOOs, and MUDs), asynchronous technologies (such as e-mail), integrated courseware programs (such as WebCT or Blackboard, programs that integrate HTML, word processing, and synchronous and asynchronous technologies), and even specially designed programs that facilitate peer review (such as CommonSpace, Webconnect, and Calibrated Peer Review™). Given this range of technologies, virtual peer review is not bound by time in the same way that face-to-face peer review is—rather, it varies in terms of what Kaufer and Carley have called "synchronicity." That is, because conversations occur through computer-mediated communication rather than through immediate face-to-face settings, virtual peer review could occur through "real-time," synchronous discussions or through delayed, asynchronous discussions.

That said, however, there are important time differences between asynchronous and synchronous applications of virtual peer review. It could be argued that both forms of technology are delayed, as does Pierre Dillenbourg, who suggests that even synchronous technology has a bit of a delay, ranging from two seconds to up to a minute. He asks, "Where is the threshold beyond which one considers communication to be asynchronous?" (12). Considering the slight delay of synchronous technologies, I would argue that even synchronous technologies are not quite the same as immediate, face-to-face interaction. Students conducting virtual peer review synchronously, however, can work towards the *semblance* of a live chat, even though contributions to the online dialogue may appear disjointed. For example, Geoffrey Sirc and Tom Reynolds indicate their surprise regarding the amount of off-task talk and disjointed conversation that occurs in synchronous chats of basic writers. Because contributions to synchronous chats are slowed by technology, resulting conversations may appear differently than they would in face-to-face environments. One of the benefits, however, of using synchronous chats for virtual peer review is that participants can archive their discussion with peers to better recall the suggestions that were provided. As Eric Crump suggests, "Natural oral fluency, usually ephemeral, is now capturable" (183).

In conducting virtual peer review using synchronous technologies (such as online chats), authors must approach peer review by reading one another's writing in advance, and then meet in an online space to discuss each other's writing. Conducting virtual peer review in this way allows for instant feedback and interaction among authors; they can ask questions of one another and brainstorm ideas and suggestions for revision. If conducted in groups, reviewers can share and compare their feedback for the author all at once rather than individually (Crump; Sirc and Reynolds). Virtual peer review that uses synchronous technology thus allows for more immediate interaction between participants. Kaufer and Carley describe this interaction in terms of "reciprocity," which they associate with the term "concurrency," or the suggestion that communication occurs more or less at the same time (152–53): "Concurrency, and the ability of individuals to learn and continue to create communications, mean that there is a certain reciprocity among communication partners insofar as they continue over time to adapt to one another" (154).

If virtual peer review is conducted through asynchronous technologies (such as e-mail), time delay becomes more of an issue, and authors need to prepare for the activity differently. Instead of gathering in virtual environments for a discussion, asynchronous virtual peer review lends itself to separate reviews, timed differently. Comments tend to be less interactive and more global. Muriel Harris explains: "E-mail usually results in a nonsynchronous interaction and delays in getting a response, and it requires that the student submit an entire paper if there are larger questions about the whole text" ("Using Computers" 7). Although asynchronous technologies delay response, there are certain advantages to this change of time. For example, Kaufer and Carley specifically address asynchronous interactions in terms of the concept of *durability,* or the amount of time that a message can be responded to (102). They suggest that asynchronous interactions are more durable, because they increase the amount of time for response.

> . . . a durable communication can be received by different individuals at different times without composing secondary, tertiary, and n-level mediating communications. A durable text can continue to diffuse information through primary communication with readers even while some of these readers (e.g., reviewers, scholars, etc.) are composing secondary communications to sustain the content of the primary communication. (102–03)

Asynchronous interactions may thus be more "durable" and allow reviewers to think more carefully about their responses. Joseph Walther notes that having more time to respond allows for more reflection: "With more time for message construction and less stress of ongoing interaction, users may have taken the opportunity for objective self-awareness, reflection, selection and transmission of preferable cues" (qtd. in Walther 19). Asynchronous or delayed interactions, then, alter the immediacy associated with face-to-face peer review. Rather than responding at the same time, multiple reviewers respond on their own time, and authors may receive feedback incrementally rather than all at once. Walther argues that delayed interactions to some degree "free" participants: "[F]reed from communicating in real time, users are released from the pressure to meet and the stress of including both task and social issues in limited time intervals typically allowed by FtF interaction. Time is frozen and conversation is disentrained when partners 'meet' independent of one another" (29). Walther also notes that this feature may be very convenient: "When communication does not require [a] partner's simultaneous attention, individuals take part in their group's activities at time intervals of their own convenience. They may do so when the clock on other activities has stopped" (24).

In considering virtual peer review in classroom settings, then, an advantage of delayed interaction is that students are not restricted to classroom time limits (fifty or seventy-five minutes). Consider how many times peer review workshops may run over a specified class period, or when someone's paper doesn't get reviewed. Asynchronous interactions remove this constraint from peer review, which may benefit some reviewers and encourage them to respond more thoroughly to an author's text (Walther 24). The response from a peer reviewer in a virtual environment illustrates the benefit of "extra" time, shown in figure 2. Note that the reviewer here writes complete sentences and fleshes out thoughts and suggestions for revision. This reviewer is obviously responding to prompts given by the instructor for the peer review, but interestingly has retyped them in his or her response. The appearance of the text is neat (typewritten), and the reviewer offers many helpful suggestions. Consider the response to question number 3, which offers a critique and helpful suggestion for incorporating sources in the author's text. This virtual peer response definitely illustrates how delayed interaction can lead to thoughtful reflection.

While delayed interactions can be seen as an advantage, they can also be a disadvantage if students have a time limit for completing virtual peer review, and do not follow that time line. Consider the apologetic message from a peer reviewer who was not able to complete a review on time, shown in figure 3.

As this example shows, time is still a factor of virtual peer review, but what happens is that time becomes negotiated by the student in the virtual space rather than negotiated by an instructor or a class structure. It is an important factor for course design; in considering whether or not to use virtual peer review, instructors must decide whether or not they want students to leave with a peer review completed, or if they are willing to let students complete peer reviews on their own without the class structure. In the latter case, instructors must be willing to let go of directing peer review exercises and truly place the experience in the students' hands.

Space

Considering space leads to the concept of "presence." A frequent criticism of virtual environments is the absence of physical presence. Sometimes, however, the lack of *physical* presence is confused with lack of presence entirely. It is not that people working online are not "present," it is just that they are not directly in front of each other. Instead of physical presence, presence in

---

Author:

Reviewer:

To the reviewer: Comment on the following parts of the assignment:

1. What is the definition of sustainable agriculture offered in the reflective writing? List it here.

   The ideal sustainable agriculture is which the well being of the farm, the farmers, and the livestock is the priority maintained by an integration of sophisticated technology to maximize productivity.

2. How has the writer supported his or her definition (through an example, quotation, readings)? Explain how the writer supported his or her definition.

   There were no quotations or examples from the readings, but the author did support her idea in her introduction and body of the essay. The author first discusses that there are two sides debatable in agriculture which both have their good points. Then, the author discusses how science, naturalists, and technology affect the ecosystem and how all of it should be integrated to accomplish a common goal.

3. Has the writer included credible and relevant sources and citations? If so, list one of the sources used. If not, comment on a good place where a source could be added.

   There were no citations. A good place to place to add a source is in the paragraph explaining how every organism on this planet is interrelated with one another in a direct or indirect way. The source could further show the complicated web how every thing is chained together.

4. What style of documentation is the writer using? Provide an example of the in-text citation style used by the author.

   There was no in-text citation present. I am unsure about the documentation style, but I would guess MLA format.

5. Has the writer used correct grammar, punctuation, and spelling? If not, point out one sentence where some improvement is needed.

   Most of the paper was written pretty well. There was one sentence that needed commas shown in the following: "Technology, on the other hand, believes in controlled environment. There were no serious spelling errors, and punctuation was fine.

6. Is the organization easy to follow (are paragraphs organized logically)? Provide an example of a strong topic sentence.

   The organization was logically explained and not hard to follow. "There are two revolutions in agriculture today, both having their supporters and dissenters".

Figure 2. Asynchronous Virtual Peer Review Comments

virtual environments is created through other means. Laura Gurak discusses the lack of physical presence in terms of Internet communities, but argues that two rhetorical concepts, ethos and delivery, still create an individual presence online: ". . . community ethos and the novel mode of delivery on computer networks, are critical to rhetorical online communities because

<u>Post</u> | <u>Reply</u> | <u>Reply/Quote</u> | <u>Email Reply</u> | <u>Delete</u> | <u>Edit</u> | <u>Move</u>
<u>Previous</u> | <u>Next</u> | Previous Topic | <u>Next Topic</u> | <u>Entire Topic</u>

    Topic: Biotech assignment (2 of 2), Read 7 times
    Conf: <u>Group 6 (Mpls)</u>
    From: <u>0008@umn.edu</u>
    Date: Monday, February 21, 2000 02:18 PM

I am so sorry that I haven't gotten back to you until now. I broke my toe on friday and haven't been able to hobble to campus to use a computer, not to mention the fact that I've been so doped up on painkillers i couldn;t read the article until now. I plan to write the paper by hand tonight, email it to you tomorrow and hand it in in class. If you think there are things that should be changed, I'm sure we will be able to get some sort of an extension on account of my gimpiness.

Figure 3. Virtual Peer Reviewer Comment on Time

these features sustain the community and its motive for action in the absence of physical commonality or traditional face-to-face methods of establishing presence and delivering a message" (*Persuasion and Privacy* 5).

In addition, several scholars in computer-mediated communication have explained that in virtual environments, presence is further altered because social cues such as race, gender, and status fall away (Lea and Spears, "Paralanguage"; Hiltz and Turoff; Walther). As Martin Lea and Russell Spears put it, computer-mediated communication "filters out many of the social and affective cues associated with human interaction" ("Paralanguage" 321). In using the word "filter," Lea and Spears remind us that social cues are not *eliminated* in virtual environments (as critics might argue) but that they are *reduced*. They argue that the cues remaining in virtual environments—cues that may include paralinguistic marks and tonality of text—take on even greater importance (see also Walther). The activity of virtual peer review, conducted in virtual spaces, means that participants are not physically present, but that they are limited to the social cues they can create in the virtual environment.

However, the filtering of social cues in the virtual environment has led to inferences that virtual spaces are less personal—even, as Walther has phrased it, "impersonal" (7). This characterization has appeared in accounts of online tutoring. For instance, Scott Russell suggests that using computers for tutoring is a dehumanizing practice ("so like a television") (72). Intrigued by claims of this sort, Walther suggests three ways to describe the affect of virtual environments: impersonal, interpersonal, and hyperpersonal. He reports that scholars in computer-mediated communication (CMC) offer conflicting accounts of how CMC reflects these qualities, and he ultimately argues that we need to reconsider suggestions that CMC does not foster personal connections. Regarding the "impersonality," Walther explains that early research on computer-mediated communication suggested that task was emphasized above personality. "Impersonality," he asserts, "was an effect of the lack of nonverbal cues and, at times, the reduced interactivity of e-mail and computer conferencing systems" (7). In regard to interpersonal qualities, Walther argues that communication over time develops a kind of relationship between participants. But unlike those who suggest that virtual environments do not foster interpersonal behaviors at all, Walther suggests that interpersonal relationships do develop, but that they are "temporally retarded" (10). What is meant by this is that exchanges in computer-mediated communication occur at a slower rate than they do in face-to-face environments:

> The key difference between [interpersonal] processes in CMC and FtF communication has not to do with the *amount* of social information exchanged but with the *rate* of social information exchange. This framework acknowledges that there is less social information per message in CMC because of the absence of nonverbal cues. It also recognizes the potential for users to adapt to the linguistic code as the sole channel for relational communication and refers to a number of verbal strategies in the impression formation and interpersonal interaction literature known to affect interpersonal attribution. (10; italics his)

Finally, regarding the hyperpersonal, Walther argues that online environments may encourage personal behaviors above and beyond what face-to-face environments can offer. He defines hyperpersonal as "CMC that is more socially desirable than we tend to experience in parallel FtF interaction" (17), and uses examples such as chats, bulletin boards, and games that occur in virtual environments, in which participants form particularly strong bonds with one another. The framework of impersonal, interpersonal, and hyperpersonal that Walther offers is helpful when we consider the separate space of virtual environments. Walther reminds us not to assume that absence of physical space necessarily means lack of personal connection—just that such connections may develop in different ways, bound by limited social cues over distance and time. Inae Kang applies Walther's framework to investigate the potential of computer-mediated communication for instructional environments. The results of her empirical study suggest that the integration of CMC into instructional environments has refuted claims that virtual environments are impersonal (333). She suggests that "it is not important whether CMC is impersonal or not, but, rather, how to utilize CMC for the purpose of learner-centered educational environments" (334). In her estimation, the value of CMC is that it "endorses both task-oriented and socially oriented exchanges without the limitation of time and geographical location" (334).

As we consider the issue of space—specifically, the absence of a physical presence—in terms of virtual peer review, there are a number of factors to keep in mind. First, authors may hold the same biases against virtual environments that have been articulated in the literature, such as the idea that virtual spaces are less human or personal than face-to-face meetings. Consider the comment from a student in a peer review group about using online spaces, shown in figure 4. And yet, students may find, as Inae Kang reported, that virtual spaces lend themselves well to task completion as well as to discussion about ideas. Consider the responses to this student's message, shown in figures 5 and 6. What is interesting about these passages is that students here are establishing the virtual space in their own terms, personalizing it, if you will, for their group interactions to come. In the second response, the student encourages her group to continue the conversation about their course content "no matter how"—meaning that she believes the discussion is important to have, whether that occurs in person or in virtual space.

In addition to attitudes about the absence of physical space, there are two other factors to consider regarding space and virtual peer review. First, it may be more helpful for virtual peer review to involve the same participants for every peer review session than to have different groups for peer review. Second, it would be helpful to assign virtual peer review groups to work with

---

<u>TOP</u> | <u>Post</u> | <u>Reply</u> | <u>Reply/Quote</u> | <u>Email Reply</u> | <u>Delete</u> | <u>Edit</u> | <u>Move</u>
Previous | Next | Previous Topic | Next Topic | Entire Topic

    Topic: GREAT (1 of 2), Read 19 times
    Conf: <u>Group 1 (St. Paul)</u>
    From: <u>0004@umn.edu</u>
    Date: Tuesday, February 15, 2000 03:09 PM

Wow! This webboard thing is really cool. I can just sit here and type tons of crap in here and no one knows when I am being sarcastic! I love being alienated even further from interpersonal communication by this wonderful technology. Is there anyone out there who would even think of questioning its use in all facets of our life? I surely think not! This is better than interpersonal communication any day. I love not ever seeing the faces of the people in class. The TV's help out with that as well, because the 2-D images can give us distance and help us objectify our peers. The best part of all of this has to be the abolition of the joys of warm, living, direct experience when communicating with other people.

Sarcastically ???, yours,

Figure 4. Virtual Peer Reviewer Comment on Online Space

Post | Reply | Reply/Quote | Email Reply | Delete | Edit | Move
Previous | Next | Previous Topic | Next Topic | Entire Topic

Topic: GREAT (2 of 2), Read 16 times
Conf: Group 1 (St. Paul)
From: 0042@umn.edu
Date: Saturday, February 19, 2000 01:48 PM

Yeah, this webboard thing is a cheap imitation of real interpersonal communication, but it sure works great when everyone is on different rhythm

Post New Topic | Reply to: "GREAT"

Figure 5. Virtual Peer Reviewer Comment on Online Space

Post | Reply | Reply/Quote | Email Reply | Delete | Edit | Move
Previous | Next | Previous Topic | Next Topic | Entire Topic

Topic: Wonderful (1 of 1), Read 44 times
Conf: Welcome!
From: 0005@umn.edu
Date: Thursday, February 17, 2000 01:08 PM

Yes, computer technology is great i agree with [g]. Now each of us can complacently sit by and have absolutely no control over the direction of our society. Put it in the hands of rich white guys out for profit and not for the earth's welfare to craft the map of our future. Gosh, I love not knowing whether our children's future will be at all worth living if to only live in further domination.
Come on people we must talk openly about these issues - of consumption, capitalism, our pseudo-democracy, our feel-good environmentalism, and many more things that are tucked away in the hidden folds of what is not reported to us daily by the media - cause there's only a few media engines now to control what we see and hear everyday.
I want dialogue - I want people to wake up, look people in the eye, and realize we are not supreme beings here.
Please respond, whatever way. I am not trying to be confrontational with any particular beliefs, I just want the truth, as   does too. I mean, if this class is about the env't, the citizen(us) and global food production, then this dialogue should happen.

Figure 6. Virtual Peer Reviewer Comment on Online Space

each other for long periods of time—such as over a semester, rather than over a few weeks. If we agree with Walther that interpersonal behaviors occur in virtual environments, but that they are "temporally retarded," it makes sense to create virtual peer review groups that would function over a long term rather than over the short term. This structure would give authors the opportunity to continue working with one another over time and maximize the virtual environment for both task and interpersonal behaviors.

Interaction

Last but certainly not least, an important difference of virtual peer review is that interactions are text-based, rather than speech-based. Because virtual peer review is conducted entirely online, all activities—such as writing documents, exchanging documents, and conversing about documents—occur via written interactions. William Condon suggests that this shift to text-based interactions makes virtual classrooms "a written classroom, not just a writing classroom" (49). The same is true of virtual peer review; that is, virtual peer review becomes an exercise of writing rather than an exercise of speaking. As several scholars have pointed out, the primary advantage of this environment for writing instruction is that text-only environments reinforce the writing act. Harris and Pemberton suggest, for example, that "to use the system, students must do the one thing we work hardest to get them to do: write. They must not only reflect upon their texts and respond to our questions; they must do so by composing, by putting their thoughts and ideas into written form" (154; see also Jordan-Henley and Maid 212; Berge and Collins 4). Condon also suggests that text-only environments encourage student development: "Virtual space may be hard to locate, but it provides a powerful environment for helping students see themselves as writers, for helping them understand all that is involved in addressing an audience, and for helping them see how multifaceted a thing writing in any context really is" (50).

While virtual environments encourage students to write, the issue, in terms of virtual peer review, becomes one of how students *respond* in writing. That is, how well do they convey (in text) their suggestions, comments, and questions to fellow students? Does the virtual environment stifle response in any way? The answer to these questions is that response depends on a number of factors: the context, the reviewer, the purpose of the review, and so on. But certainly, text-only environments need not stifle peer review response. In fact, they can draw out response more fully. As Barbara Monroe suggests, text-only comments can be shaped to reflect both intertextual commentary and interpersonal commentary. In "The Look and Feel of the OWL Conference," Monroe describes how online tutors can respond to students in the virtual environment. She introduces a taxonomy for text-based comments that includes "front comments," "intertextual comments," and "end comments." Front comments, she suggests, are much like a personal note from a tutor to a student, explaining how the tutor will respond to his or her text and what textual cues to look for (i.e., "my comments will be in BOLD throughout your paper") (7). Intertextual comments are found throughout a document and may be signaled by the tutor in some way using a symbol (15). For example, in figure 7, a student used a hash mark (###) to signal intertextual comments. Intertextual comments may reflect reactions, suggestions, or criticisms from the reader, and they are helpful in addressing specific sections of the text.

End comments, according to Monroe, are found at the end of a document, often in summary fashion and often focusing on global features of the text (22). An example of an endnote can be seen in figure 8. Note that end comments can be quite comprehensive, reflecting summary comments from a reviewer and providing suggestions in detail for the author. While this structure proposed by Monroe (front, intertextual, and end comments) is a useful model that demonstrates how students can approach response in virtual environments, some would no doubt argue that text-only comments are less beneficial than oral response. For example, in "The Language of Writing Groups," Gere and Stevens argue that face-to-face environments encourage "genuine" response to student texts. They picture an environment in which authors read their texts out loud to a group of peer reviewers, and that reviewers can chime in at certain points with questions or comments, giving immediate feedback to authors from readers' perspectives. Interestingly, Gere and

> The other options to on-campus housing of animals might include
>off-campus
>farms, however, this would be inefficient to the University.
>Students would have to travel to off-campus farms, which would use up
>too much time in a student's already busy daily schedule. True, the
>smell of the composting would be less but the time factor is too great
>to even consider this option.
####May want to talk about smell and what can be done, also how it would

effect cost
>   The responsibility of animal waste disposal should lie within
>the facilities and agricultural management of the University of Minnesota.
> The general University fund should be responsible for the payments
and

Figure 7. Intertextual Comments in Virtual Peer Review

Stevens compare this student-group feedback—oral and dynamic—with teacher feedback on student writing, which tends to be "fixed," written, and in one chunk: "[T]eacher responses are highly generalized. They thus lack that focus on the text which we find in the language of writing groups and do not constitute a genuine reaction or response" (97). Gere and Stevens make the excellent point that the type of response in oral peer review groups is immediate and focused on the text in comparison with teacher comments. However, when we observe written comments in virtual peer review, they are no less text-focused, and perhaps, it could be argued, *more* text focused. That is, because virtual peer reviewers focus on reading and responding to an author's writing, they become somewhat closer to the text than they might in a face-to-face encounter. The roles become interchanged between reader and writer, but are always text-based.

Although these few examples may illustrate how response looks and appears differently in the virtual environment, much more research needs to be conducted to investigate the quality of text-only responses or patterns of text-based response that may occur. Future studies might address, for example, a

---

Just a few suggestions . . . You already realize that the paper should be memo format, I would suggest beginning with the second paragraph for this format. You may use the existing first paragraph in a different place, if you want. Basically, a memo does not need an introductory section of information on the topic. It is assumed that the reader is familiar with the topic at hand.

Keep in mind the 3 questions in the assignment. The grade is based on answering those questions in a clear and concise manner. You may want to look over those questions and answer them more clearly. I couldn't tell who you think should pay for the waste disposal, who is responsible . . . The first two questions you addressed very well, but question 3 could use more work.

I like your technical knowledge in the paper, however, you may want to consider showing some solutions on how to control the smell factor, who would pay, (basically refer to the assigned questions . . .)

I liked the paragraph explaining that "animal waste is not as dangerous as chemical, hazardous, . . . etc. . ." I also liked the closing point that an experimental station needs to use manure and other fertilizer (check your spelling of fertilizer) but refocuses on how to dispose of excess manure (solutions).

I hope my suggestions help. If you want to email a second draft, feel free. I will be checking my email regularly in the next few days. If you want to call me that is OK too . . . I should be home studying, (what else do I ever do?)

Figure 8. Virtual Peer Review "Endnote"

Table 2

Characteristics of Virtual Peer Review

	Definition	*Virtual Peer Review*
Time		
Synchronicity	Time varies from immediate response to delayed response	Virtual peer reviewers have option of synchronous or asynchronous response
Durability	Written communication remains durable over time	An author's writing and a reviewer's feedback are both "durable" when conducted via technology; asynchronous messages and synchronous chats can be saved and transferred intact
Concurrency	Responses occur more or less at the same time	Virtual peer review encourages continued response
Convenience	Time restrictions are lifted to some degree	Virtual peer review can be conducted on one's own time; extra time can be used for greater reflection if needed; reviewers must be disciplined
Space		
Social Cues	Race, class, and gender are no longer immediately visible	Removal of social cues encourages virtual peer reviewers to focus on the task at hand
Interpersonal presence	Interpersonal connections often take longer to foster online	Virtual peer reviewers may develop interpersonal ties over time when working together in a group
Hyperpersonal presence	Connections that are more intense than in face-to-face situations	Virtual peer review may result in stronger interpersonal connections and presence online between reviewers

(continued on next page)

Table 2 *(continued)*

	Definition	*Virtual Peer Review*
Interaction		
Text-based	Online communication encourages increased writing practice	Virtual peer review encourages writing, not only through the creation of documents but through written response to one another, either synchronously or asynchronously
Fixity	Written communication becomes "fixed" online	Virtual peer review comments can be archived and saved to stimulate recall of peer suggestions and revisions
Response structure	Online communication can take form of front, intertextual, and end comments	Virtual peer review can be tailored to provide summary comments, intertextual comments on specific passages, or overall discussion about an author's questions or problem areas
Reach	Preservation of accuracy of message	Comments from virtual peer reviewers are preserved intact and can be transmitted to multiple audiences

concept called "reach," which Kaufer and Carley identify as the number of people within a society who actually receive the message. They suggest that reach can be addressed socially, in terms of how many people receive a message, and cognitively, in terms of how accurately information is grasped and by whom. To illustrate reach, Kaufer and Carley use the example of a gossip who may spread information to many people but diminish the accuracy of the message (126–27). Some might argue that face-to-face interactions lead to more "reach"—that is, that face-to-face interaction leads to a better understanding of reviewer comments and response, because reviewers can discuss points further. Yet, because virtual peer review involves durable messages and reviewer comments are printed and can be easily delivered (intact), it could be argued that in terms of accuracy "reach" is greater in virtual peer review than in face-to-face peer review. Again, pursuing this line of inquiry would require much more research and investigation.

While the benefit of text-based comments in virtual peer review could be argued (infinitely, perhaps), one clear advantage of text-based interactions for virtual peer review is that students then have a permanent record of their reviewer's comments. Kaufer and Carley refer to this quality of text-based interactions as "fixity," or "the degree to which communication technology enables the communication to be retransmitted without change" (100). They assert that "fixity is a property of a communication technology," and that is certainly the case in terms of virtual peer review, which relies on Internet technology for exchange and correspondence. In virtual peer review, students can archive written comments of reviewers for future reference as they revise their work. When peer review is conducted in groups, this feature is especially useful, because students can categorize comments according to author. In addition, comments can be made available for instructors to review. These advantages would not exist in face-to-face peer review environments; students may not remember all comments that students offer, and instructors seldom have the opportunity to examine comments offered by peer reviewers.

As I have demonstrated in this chapter, even though virtual peer review and nonvirtual peer review share similar definitions and have similar pedagogical assumptions as peer review, virtual peer review has important characteristics that differ from peer review in terms of time, space, and interaction. These characteristics, summarized in table 2, illuminate ways that peer review changes when conducted through computer technology.

Identifying these characteristics allows us to begin identifying the remediation of peer review in virtual environments. Simply put, virtual peer review as a remediation can be best described by the ways computer technology privileges written communication over oral communication—a flip-flop of how peer review has traditionally been discussed in writing studies. Although this full reversal may be easily assimilated in some settings (such as workplaces or academic publishing, which frequently require cross-country collaboration or review processes), a greater tension surrounds this reversal in writing studies, particularly in writing instruction, where peer review is frequently conducted in face-to-face workshops. As I discuss in the next chapter, this tension is exacerbated by the connection several scholars have made between peer review and social theories of language that privilege oral over written communication.

To investigate this tension more fully, in the next chapter I work through issues that surface in moving peer review to virtual environments, and I argue that writing studies can benefit from assimilating virtual peer review in instructional practices. Specifically, including virtual peer review in teaching practices expands our notions of "conversation" and "dialogue" to embrace written interactions, helps student writers embrace computer technology more fully, and helps writers practice and strengthen written response and review.

CHAPTER 3

Virtual Peer Review
as Abnormal Discourse

As the last chapter has demonstrated, the introduction of computer technology means that virtual peer review is primarily an exercise in writing rather than an exercise in speaking. As such, it takes on characteristics that are different from those in face-to-face peer review in terms of time, space, and interaction. In this chapter, I suggest that while this remediation of peer review opens the door to many benefits, such as convenience, increased writing practice, and increased durability of peer comments, many writing instructors still resist virtual peer review. A primary reason for this resistance, I believe, is that peer review has been documented in scholarship as a speech-based instructional activity. That is, peer review at its very core involves social interaction, but most research about peer review has thus far been grounded in face-to-face environments in which oral communication, not written communication, prevails. In addition, research about peer review has been reinforced by a significant body of research about face-to-face interactions in composition, such as teacher-student inter-actions (Sperling; Freedman and Katz; Black; Harris, *Teaching*), student-student interactions (Gere and Stevens; Burnett, "Interactions"; Wallace), and tutor-student interactions (Reigstad and McAndrew; B. L. Clark; Shamoon and Burns). Because peer review has such a documented history in oral com-munication, the revival of writing in peer review through computer technology appears to me an intriguing case study of sorts: one in which we can examine intersecting tensions that surround the remediation of speech-based activities to computer-based activities.

In this chapter, then, I investigate the tension that may result from the suggestion that peer review be extended to include computer-mediated com-munication, as well as face-to-face interaction. In exploring this tension, I for-ward the argument that this seemingly logical extension carries with it marks of what Rorty has called "abnormal discourse," or discourse that pushes boundaries of normal or accepted disciplinary conventions (*Philosophy* 320). That is, expanding an activity we have come to associate with oral communi-cation to computer environments in many ways seems off-the-wall and not within our "normal" understanding of peer review. In considering an expan-sion of peer review to include its virtual enactment, I argue that we frequently confront classifications of inferiority and superiority ("f2f is better than virtual peer review"), or misperceptions that virtual peer review would replace f2f peer review ("the computer is no replacement for *human* interaction"). In response, I suggest that as a remediation, virtual peer review does not at all change the solid pedagogical assumptions that inform peer review as an instructional activity: as I have explained, virtual peer review upholds assumptions that writing is a process, that writing is student-centered, and that writing is a social act. What changes is the *practice* of the activity, which means that peer review is conducted differently in terms of time, space, and interaction. I suggest that these differences of time, space, and interaction in the virtual environment have not been discussed enough to be accepted in the "normal" discourse of peer review, and thus are often treated with suspicion. Virtual peer review exemplifies, on a small scale, the tension we may feel regarding classroom activities or assignments moving to virtual environments.

My purpose in this chapter is to try to make sense of this tension—where it is originating and how best to acknowledge, yet move past, this tension to embrace virtual environments for peer review. I begin by framing the tension in terms of "normal" and "abnormal" discourse, and to explicate these terms I turn to the work of Thomas Kuhn, Richard Rorty, and Kenneth Bruffee. Next, I suggest that the normal discourse of peer review is speech-based interactions, because of the associations with social theories of language that emphasize the primacy of speech. Finally, I suggest that breaking into the normal discourse of peer review requires a reconsideration of both the hierarchy and separation of speech and writing, thus pushing toward a "new dimension" defined by literacy activities of reading, writing, and interacting online.

Normal and Abnormal Discourse

The terms "normal discourse" and "abnormal discourse" refer to, respectively, accepted theories, conventions, or observations of an academic community, and unconventional theories or observations that push the boundaries of what is accepted. The terms are reminiscent of Thomas Kuhn's landmark essay, *The Structure of Scientific Revolutions,* in which Kuhn discusses the evolution of new theories or scientific facts within scientific communities, a process that tests what he calls "normal science." According to Kuhn, normal science represents accepted scientific theorems or facts as well as an acknowledgment of what is acceptable science. He writes that normal science "means research firmly based upon one or more past scientific achievements, achievements that some particular scientific community acknowledges for a time as supplying the foundation for its further practice" (10). Kuhn explains that normal science—a term he closely associates with "paradigm" (10)—is used to solve scientific problems. The inability of normal science to solve problems causes a shift—what, since then, has been commonly referred to as a "paradigm shift." Paradigm shifts occur when scientists discover new ways to address problems that are no longer consistent with normal science. The consummate example of such a paradigm shift is the Copernican revolution, or the discovery that the earth is not the center of the universe, but that the earth and planets revolve around the sun. Kuhn is interested in exploring the historical side to scientific thought; that is, not just the emergence of new facts, observations, or experiments, but how scientific communities establish and reestablish normal science within their communities.

Richard Rorty, citing Kuhn, employs the terms "normal discourse" and "abnormal discourse" to address not only scientific discourse, but discourse on a broader scale (*Philosophy* 333). As he explains:

> [N]ormal discourse is that which is conducted within an agreed-upon set of conventions about what counts as a relevant contribution, what counts as answering a question, what counts as having a good argument for that answer or a good criticism of it. Abnormal discourse is what happens when someone joins in the discourse who is ignorant of these conventions or who sets them aside. (320)

Rorty aims to address normal and abnormal discourse from a hermeneutic perspective, and I find particularly useful his discussion of these terms in *Philosophy and the Mirror of Nature*. In this book, Rorty connects the terms normal and abnormal discourse to a distinction between epistemology and hermeneutics, which he describes as the following: "[H]ermeneutics is, roughly, a description of our study of the unfamiliar and epistemology is, roughly, a description of our study of the familiar" (353). He suggests that normal discourse reflects epistemology or agreed-upon accounts (what he associates with Davidson's "conceptual scheme" [347]), whereas abnormal discourse reflects hermeneutics or our best attempts to "cope" with accounts that cannot be explained by our normal discourse (356). Rorty frequently suggests that normal discourse consists of an established vocabulary for discourse but that abnormal discourse occurs when we do not have vocabulary for description. He argues that normal and abnormal discourse do not necessarily compete with one another, "but rather help each other out" (346).

I find Rorty's account of normal and abnormal discourse—and respective associations with epistemology and hermeneutics—quite useful in relation to peer review and virtual peer review. As I argue in the following section, most accounts of peer review reflect face-to-face environments, and volumes of research about speech interactions reinforce these accounts—what I am calling the normal discourse of peer review. Virtual peer review differs markedly from the face-to-face interactions so often recorded in peer review literature. My efforts to name the differences in terms of time, space, and interaction are an effort to cope with the lack of appropriate vocabulary to describe how peer review can occur in virtual environments.

It is important to note that my application of the terms "normal" and "abnormal" discourse to peer review is not original—Bruffee also employed the terms in his support of collaborative learning. But he did so in a much different way, relying on normal discourse rather than on abnormal discourse to support collaborative learning and peer review. In "Collaboration and the 'Conversation of Mankind,'" Bruffee argues that collaborative learning is a pedagogical technique that encourages the reinforcement of normal discourse in any discipline. Borrowing Rorty's use of the term, he explains normal discourse as a commonly accepted set of conventions in a discipline; those who articulate and work within those conventions through oral or written communication demonstrate their solidarity within a community (642–43). Bruffee suggests that collaborative learning, through its encouragement of student conversation and work in small groups, is a way to model "the kind of community in which normal discourse occurs: a community of knowledgeable peers" (644). Bruffee asserts that, as a form of collaborative learning, peer review (or peer critique or evaluation, as he calls it), also reinforces normal discourse. In this way, Bruffee relies heavily on the concept of normal discourse to justify collaborative learning. In addition, he perhaps has larger goals than I have with regard to virtual peer review. That is, Bruffee is ultimately concerned with forwarding "nonfoundational" approaches to knowledge, and he maintains that social discourse—or conversation—plays a role in the construction of knowledge and the maintenance of communities. It is less clear how abnormal discourse fits in with Bruffee's advocacy of collaborative learning or peer review. Interestingly, Bruffee revised the term "abnormal discourse" in his 1999 publication of *Collaborative Learning*. Instead of "abnormal discourse" he uses the term "nonstandard, boundary discourse" (143), and applies it in reference to the role of conversation in the construction of knowledge in academic communities. He does not apply nonstandard discourse directly to peer review but rather to academic communities: "Nonstandard discourse [. . .] occurs at the boundaries of established knowledge communities in ad hoc transition groups where the standards of no established community prevail" (143). Bruffee is concerned with—on a much larger scale—the use of nonstandard or abnormal discourse to describe the social construction of academic conventions and communities.

In my treatment of peer review, I rely more heavily on abnormal discourse than does Bruffee, and I apply the term in a more local way to explain the tension that exists within our normal discourse of peer review when considering virtual environments for peer review. Through this approach, I am suggesting that the differences of time, space, and interaction that occur in virtual environments for peer review do not fit our normal discourse of peer review, and consequently rely on our hermeneutic ability to assimilate them into our understanding of peer review. Given this background, in the next section I explain the normal discourse of peer review as situated in speech-based, face-to-face environments.

Normal Discourse of Peer Review: Oral Communication

My claim that peer review is primarily based in face-to-face environments (creating a "normal discourse" for the activity of peer review) requires a reexamination of the association of peer review with social theories of language. In chapter 1 I suggested that one assumption of peer review is that writing is a social act, and I briefly reviewed the work of Gere and others who have suggested that peer review reinforces social theories of language such as those espoused by Vygotsky and Bakhtin. Here I devote much more attention to this connection, for it represents, in my opinion, the crux of the debate regarding peer review in virtual (written) environments and peer review in face-to-face (oral) environments. While social theories of language (those of Vygotsky and Bakhtin, in particular) account for both oral and written communication, they highlight the primacy of oral communication in understanding the social construction of knowledge. I argue that when these theories have been applied to peer review, the same primacy of oral communication is reflected. For example, terms that have often been employed to describe peer review include "conversation" and "dialogue," and research about peer review predominantly includes transcripts of oral dialogues (Gere and Stevens). In the following paragraphs I review the work of Vygotsky, Bakhtin, and Bruffee regarding distinctions of oral and written communication (including terms such as "conversation" and "dialogue"). I then suggest that while these distinctions have been used as a basis to support peer review as a pedagogical activity, most research about peer review practice and related activities within the past two decades privileges oral communication and face-to-face environments for the activity of responding to one another's writing. This primacy of oral communication creates what I call a "normal discourse" for the activity of peer review, and as I suggest in the following sections, it exists in both peer review theory and practice.

Normal Discourse in Peer Review Theory

It is important to first review in greater detail social theories of language that have been invoked in support of peer review as a pedagogical activity. Let me begin by reviewing the concept of "inner speech" from Vygotsky's *Thought and Language*. Vygotsky argues, unlike Piaget, that inner speech reflects our external conversations—our social speech—rather than any individualized form of speech developed in early childhood (or "egocentric speech") (32–34). As Gere suggests, for Vygotsky individual language and social language are not isolated from one another: "[T]hey remain interlocked because individual language is internalized social language" (81–82).

The idea of inner speech is critical to the argument that writing is social, and several scholars have supported this idea. For example, Karen LeFevre invokes the idea of internalized speech to suggest that writing derives from social conversation (58). Likewise, Bruffee relies on the idea of inner speech—"conversation" in his terms—in his explanation of writing: "If thought is internalized public and social talk, then writing of all kinds is internalized social talk made public and social again. If thought is internalized conversation, then writing is internalized conversation re-externalized" (641). Bruffee clearly suggests the primacy of oral communication when he suggests that writing is "displaced conversation": "Like thought, writing is related to conversation in both time and function. Writing is a technologically displaced form of conversation. When we write, having already internalized the 'skill and partnership' of conversation, we displace it once more onto the written page" (641). Bruffee suggests, therefore, that while writing is a form of conversation (or social speech), it is secondary, for it is possible only because we already have internalized social speech based on our conversations with others.[1] Thus, Vygotsky's use of the term "inner speech" (as well as those who adopt it), stresses that social speech—in other words, orality—forms the basis of thought. I believe this demonstrates the primacy of oral communication in the act of writing, specifically that writing is based on our reflections and experience with speech situations.

This primacy of oral communication is even more pronounced in Bakhtin's description of speech genres. Indeed, Bakhtin suggests that primary speech genres, which he calls simple genres, consist of "live" communication, while secondary speech genres, which he calls complex genres, include written communication and "highly developed and organized cultural communication" (946). Bakhtin explains, in similar fashion to Vygotsky, how secondary genres are based on oral communication: "In secondary speech genres. [. . .] Quite frequently within the boundaries of his own utterance the speaker (or writer) raises questions, answers them himself, raises objections to his own ideas, responds to his own objections, and so on. But these phenomena are nothing other than a conventional playing out of oral communication and primary speech genres" (953). While Bakhtin's theory of dialogue is based primarily on oral communication (G. Clark 13), Bakhtin acknowledges that writing, too, can be a form of dialogue. For example, Bakhtin suggests that an utterance can be comprised of one spoken word, or of an entire novel. The utterance, according to Bakhtin, is a complete, expressed thought, and Bakhtin is careful to distinguish it from a sentence with syntactic structure. That is, utterances are not defined by any systematic structure, but represent a thought in an ongoing conversation. Thus, Bakhtin does not exclude written communication in his theory of dialogue; however, oral communication is clearly primary in his theory.

Because oral communication is emphasized in social theories of language presented by Vygotsky and Bakhtin, peer review scholars seem to find it especially important to highlight oral communication in the activity—perhaps to justify peer review as a sound pedagogical application of social theories of language. As I demonstrate in the next section, I believe the primacy of oral communication expressed in these theories has fostered a "normal discourse" for peer review that highlights oral communication in the activity. Indeed, scholars have *labored* to integrate oral communication into peer review and related activities. Undoing this carefully built connection would seem abnormal indeed.

Normal Discourse in Peer Review Practice

As I mentioned in chapter 2, peer review literature has mostly concentrated on face-to-face interactions, or oral communication, advocating the benefits of such interactions like immediacy of feedback, "genuine" reader response, and a sense of audience (Gere and Stevens; Spear, *Sharing Writing* 6; DiPardo and Freedman 130–33). Karen Spear suggests, in fact, that composing and "peer instruction"—a reference to talk—are "two sides of the same rhetorical coin":

> Talking, like writing, necessitates audience and purpose, discovery and "arrangement." It provides the added advantage of instant response and feedback. Thus, the act of talking is a process of discovering, articulating, and clarifying meaning based on the flow of verbal and non-verbal cues the interaction generates. (*Sharing Writing* 6)

In arguing that a normal discourse of oral communication exists for peer review, I do not suggest that writing is excluded from peer review. On the contrary, as Thom Hawkins points out, writing is an important part of peer review, especially when it provides a record of suggestions and comments offered by peers. Hawkins advocates the following steps for peer review workshops:

1. reading
2. spoken feedback,
3. written feedback. (29)

Others have also suggested ways to integrate writing in peer review. As Spear demonstrates, peers may be encouraged to write responses directly on another student's text (*Sharing Writing* 101); they may be asked to complete a worksheet of questions about their peers' texts (92–93); they may be asked to freewrite on their peer's paper as they are reading it (107). In fact, in *A Short Course in Writing*, Bruffee describes peer review—which he calls "peer criticism"—as primarily an exercise of writing, not speaking: "That peer criticism is *written* is its third important characteristic" (115, italics his). Because students write criticism directly to their peers, Bruffee describes peer criticism as "the most difficult writing any student will ever do because it is the most *real* writing most students ever do as students" (115, italics his). He suggests that peer criticism occurs in three phases: in the first phase, students describe (in writing) what another student has written; in the second phase, they evaluate (in writing) the "writing technique" of the author; in the third phase there is an oral discussion in which authors have a chance to respond to the students' critiques (118–19). Thus, Bruffee strongly suggests writing as a part of peer review.

Despite the ways writing has been integrated into peer review, it is *talking* that seems to predominantly characterize peer review. Hawkins suggests, for example, that "Spoken feedback is the spine of the workshop, the real 'work' of the hour" (29). Indeed, scholars have supported talk in peer review because of associations with social theories of language that suggest the primacy of oral communication. As Gere explains: "Vygotsky's theory thus supports the idea that talking about language in writing groups helps participants understand writing more fully" (95).

The normal discourse of oral communication in peer review is also reinforced in other types of writing conferences that involve peer review, such as writing center tutoring and teacher-student conferences. Although these types of conferences differ from peer review in terms of power differentials that may be introduced, they share the common task of responding to student writing; thus, I find them important to review here. In addition, writing conferences also support social theories of language and the idea that talking about writing is sound pedagogy. I argue that examining this literature demonstrates just how fully the normal discourse of oral communication has permeated peer review activities in writing instruction. Interestingly, the preference for oral communication in this literature is even more prevalent than the preference for oral communication in peer review. For example, teacher-student conferences have become a common (yet extremely time-consuming) practice among writing instructors as a way to talk with students about their writing. As Muriel Harris suggests in *Teaching One-to-One:*

> Conferences, opportunities for highly productive dialogues between writers and teacher-readers, are or should be an integral part of teaching writing. It

> is in the one-to-one setting of a conference that we can meet with writers
> and hear them talk about their writing. And they can also hear us talk, not
> about writing in the abstract, but about *their* writing. (3)

According to Harris, the immediate speech situation is critical to conferences, making them truly unique instructional opportunities for students. Melanie Sperling also aligns teacher-student conferences with oral communication, as she suggests in "I Want to Talk to Each of You": "We are coming to know, too, that learning to write—which is to say, acquiring and developing written language—is, as is learning to speak, a fundamentally social activity, embedded in interactions with teachers and others" (281).

Sperling's study about teacher-student conferences clearly emphasizes oral communication, in that she regularly conducts discourse analyses of oral transcripts. One study in particular, an ethnographic study on teacher-student conferences in a ninth-grade writing course, demonstrates the dynamism of teacher-student speech interactions and their effects on individual needs of students in the study. Even more striking, in *Between Talk and Teaching: Reconsidering the Writing Conference,* Laurel Johnson Black describes teacher-student conferences as "speech genres," a clear reference to Bakhtin (28). Black suggests that conferencing is a speaking experience, and in fact she includes finer distinctions between "talk" and "conversation" in conference settings. Indeed, Black's argument is that conferencing is not mere conversation, but consists of its own speech genre: "For conferencing is not a genre of speech that we are familiar with; it is something that must be learned" (28). Her project is to define more fully the speech genre of teacher-student conferences.

The normal discourse of peer review is also evident in literature about writing center conferences. However, unlike teacher-student conferences, writing center tutorials have been addressed in terms of both oral communication and written communication. That is, there is emerging literature about computer-based tutorials (*written* tutorial interactions—see Hobsen; Inman and Sewell). Despite emerging interest in these other forms of tutoring, there remains a strong preference for speech-based tutorials in writing centers. This preference may exist in part because writing center tutorials have been traditionally established in terms of speech-based interactions. Like research about teacher-student conferences, research about writing center tutorials often employs terms such as "talk" and "conversation" to describe the work of writing centers:

> Tutors use talk and questioning and all the cues they can pick up in the face-
> to-face interaction. The conversation is free to roam in whatever direction
> the student and tutor see as useful. That is, the tutor can ask about writing

habits and processes, can listen to the student's responses to various questions, and can use them as cues for further questions; and the student can express concerns not visible in the product. (Harris, "Talking" 29)

In "The Tutoring Process: Exploring Paradigms and Practices," Christina Murphy and Steve Sherwood describe tutoring in terms of dialogue:

In the tutoring session, two people work together toward a common goal; they collaborate. The purpose of the collaboration is to assist writers in their own development. The dialogue between tutor and student—a conversation with a definite purpose—is the basis upon which tutors and students build a supportive, working relationship. (1)

To some degree, the descriptors of "conversation," "talk," and "dialogue" have become associated with an interpersonal relationship between tutor and student. Like Murphy and Sherwood, Judith Powers and Jane Nelson describe tutoring in these terms: "Typically, this collaboration is described as an interchange between the writer and the writing center staff member, a one-to-one relationship" (12). (See also Harris, *Teaching;* Olson; Lunsford.) This observation of speech-based tutorials as interpersonal relationships is important with regard to a perceived lack of interpersonal connection in computer-based tutorials.

Even further evidence of the primacy of oral communication in writing center tutorials exists in the volumes of accounts of "dialogue strategies" created for tutors. For instance, in *Talking about Writing* Beverly Clark suggests ways in which tutors can foster writing center dialogues by asking questions (126), modeling (128), reading aloud (129), and "deferring to the student" (130). Many studies about one-to-one tutorials describe general prompts that can be used during tutorials for various situations. For example, in *The Practical Tutor,* Emily Meyer and Louise Z. Smith compiled the following list of questions that tutors should ask students to help them develop ideas:

General Amplification:	Tell me more about
Clarification:	I'm not sure what you mean by _______; would you explain that a bit?
Specification:	Which one did you have in mind? Where did that happen? For example? Like what? Would you give an instance, please?
Qualification:	What exceptions can you think of? When was this not true?

> Paraphrase or Summary: Let me see if I can sum up what you just said:
> In this paragraph, you said that
> You told me that (34)

A similar list of prompts is found in the strategy called "collaborative planning," a strategy that applies to peer tutoring or student-student interactions (Wallace). In collaborative planning, students converse with one another to learn about rhetorical elements in composition (audience, purpose, and context). Playing the roles of writer and supporter, students take turns asking each other questions about the audience, purpose, and context for their writing. Students who engage in collaborative planning are given lists with suggested prompts such as these:

> What do you see as your main point [purpose]?
> Who is your intended audience [reader]?
> What does the reader expect to read [learn]?
> What *support* [or evidence] will you use?
> What *examples* will you use? (Wallace 58)

The questions about writing in both of these extracts are intended to help students talk about rhetorical elements and begin to use vocabulary associated with writing studies. Although such questions could be used for written responses as well, authors of these dialogue strategies clearly emphasize the role of oral communication in peer tutoring situations.

In addition to emphasizing the role of oral communication, dialogue strategies for writing centers play a strong role in the shaping of tutor behavior. Dialogue strategies have been closely associated with tutor roles, suggesting that how a tutor *speaks* also defines that tutor's approach. For example, writing center literature is dominated by the suggestion that tutors should assume "nondirective" roles in tutorials (the student-centered model). In nondirective tutoring, tutors are discouraged from showing any kind of authority (Harris, "Talking"), such as by making suggestions on text or comments on expression or mechanics. A response to criticism that writing centers focus only on written products (student papers), nondirective tutoring models encourage a process-based approach to tutoring to help improve writers, not papers (North). In this nondirective model, then, tutors are encouraged to ask questions, listen, reflect student ideas (much like a Rogerian dialogue model in psychology), and play the role of a coach or guide for the student (B. L. Clark; Harris, *Teaching;* Harris, "Talking"). According to Beverly Clark, the role of the tutor is to ask questions that allow the student to talk and control the conversation. Clark describes this tutor dialogue strategy as serving "as a sounding board" (121). Being a sounding board means that a tutor listens, encourages talk, mirrors students thoughts, confirms problems that students sense, and even remains silent as a way to draw out student conversation (124–25). Clark likens the role of a tutor to that of Peace Corps volunteers, "who seek to make themselves dispensable, by helping their hosts to help themselves" (5). Indeed, nondirective approaches have been so frequently endorsed that Linda Shamoon and Deborah Burns refer to it as the "writing center bible" (135): "This bible contains not only the material evidence to support student-centered, non-directive practices, but also codes of behavior and statements of value that sanction tutors as a certain kind of professional, one who cares about writing and about students, their authentic voices, and their equal access to the opportunities within sometimes difficult situations" (135). Shamoon and Burns refer to nondirective approaches as the "orthodoxy [that] permeates writing center discourse" (135).

The strong support for nondirective tutoring, I believe, demonstrates a deep appreciation and even identity with oral communication, rather than written communication, in writing center tutoring—which in turn represents a full endorsement of the normal discourse I described earlier. This association may explain why some writing center scholars are skeptical and why they may strongly argue against tutoring in virtual environments. For example, in "Straddling the Virtual Fence," Eric Hobson suggests that although enthusiasm exists for online writing centers, there is an equal amount of caution about their effectiveness. In addition, affirming the speech-based, nondirective approach, Muriel Harris asserts that face-to-face environments are preferred:

> Part of tutor training is learning to listen and to engage in the kind of conversation that will help the student make such concerns explicit. Thus, since e-mail requires the writer to have some facility in question-asking, it may be an intimidating way for writers to initiate conversations with unknown, unseen tutors, especially for students at some distance from the campus who have not established a personal connection with the writing center. ("Using Computers" 7)

Harris clearly paints oral communication as the normal discourse of peer review, for she suggests that tutor training involves practice with oral communication such as listening and conversing. She further argues that, when given the choice, students will select face-to-face environments because of their preference for the "human connection" that oral communication allows, as well as the warmth of a physical environment:

> For students who do have access to the center, there is a definite preference for one-to-one meetings with tutors. In writing center evaluations, students frequently rate their experience highly because they appreciate, even welcome, the human interaction. E-mail, despite its convenience, may seem too

cold, too demanding for those students who know that they can walk over to their writing centers, almost all of which are staffed by people who have worked with great intensity and fervor to create warm, inviting environments with coffee pots steaming away, candy dishes at the reception desk, and plants and posters to advertise their student-friendly attitude. (7)

Indeed, as Harris articulates, oral communication is hailed for its potential to foster interpersonal connections with students—again, reinforcing a particular tutor approach that forms the basis of writing center philosophy. Scott Russell also expresses this hallmark of tutoring in terms of "human interaction," suggesting that oral communication facilitates "humanity" much better than computers ever could:

> The very nature of the computer screen—so like a television—calls attention to our move away from the direct human interaction that has defined our success as writing center tutors. It is important that we reconsider, in light of this trend, the human mechanics that allow for real connections in a tutorial, that we break a pattern that may have already formed instead of continuing to expanding it within the new mediums that confront us. (72)

Consider the strong resistance Russell exhibits here to virtual environments: Russell not only objects to tutoring in virtual environments, but considers it a serious mistake for the profession as a whole. Russell suggests that a move to virtual environments would not only go against the well-defined traditions established in writing center scholarship (e.g., the "writing center bible") but would abolish "human mechanics"—a suggestion that virtual environments are somehow less human than face-to-face environments. While these arguments may illustrate resistance to virtual environments in the extreme, they also clearly indicate the normal discourse of oral communication as well as efforts to preserve this normal discourse. Consequently, these arguments illustrate how online discourse—particularly written synchronous and asynchronous interactions—may appear "abnormal." In sum, I believe that writing center tutorials fully support—indeed, strengthen— the normal discourse of oral communication in the activity of peer review. However, rather than stressing the value of talk based on social theories of language, writing center scholars have done something else: They have attached value labels to oral communication. In doing so, they have endorsed the normal discourse in a way that sets up conflict with other (written) forms of peer review.

I have employed examples from teacher-student conferencing and writing center tutoring to demonstrate just how deeply the normal discourse of oral communication has permeated instructional practices related to peer review in composition. The primacy of oral communication—both in theory and practice related to peer review—may help to explain any tension that results as we consider the remediation of peer review from face-to-face to virtual interactions.

Abnormal Discourse of Virtual Peer Review: Written Communication

As I argued in chapters 1 and 2, virtual peer review shares the same pedagogical assumptions as peer review; the only significant difference is the virtual environment, which alters peer review in terms of time, space, and interaction and makes peer review an exercise in writing. In this section, I suggest how practicing peer review entirely through written communication and computers (and more importantly, instructing students to do so) may somehow feel abnormal to us. Rorty suggests that the introduction of abnormal discourse may appear either "kooky" or "revolutionary," but ultimately, abnormal discourse suggests the introduction of the unfamiliar (*Philosophy* 339).[2] Moving the interaction of peer review to virtual environments—to writing—may seem strange indeed to those of us who have been encouraged to value and practice speech interactions in our classrooms. We may, through our past training, have a solid understanding of how to organize groups, encourage certain dialogue strategies for students to respond to one another, and monitor small group peer review workshops. In short, our training may have prepared us to know a lot about *talk* in the writing classroom, and we may encourage students to talk to one another on a regular basis. We know far less about encouraging students to interact with one another *virtually* about their writing. In the next paragraphs I explore this new territory for peer review—this abnormal discourse of peer review—which endorses a fundamental shift from oral communication to written communication in the way peer review is conducted. I address this change in terms of theory and practice.

Abnormal Discourse in Virtual Peer Review Theory

A consequence of shifting peer review from oral communication to written communication is a broader interpretation of social theories of language—those of Vygotsky and Bakhtin, in particular. Although the primacy of speech was articulated by both scholars, as I suggested earlier, they both account for written communication in their theories of language development, particularly the idea that written communication reflects social speech. However, I believe this idea must be pushed further as we consider virtual environments for the activity of peer review. Specifically, in addition to acknowledging the social origins of writing, as peer review scholars have done, we must make more explicit the inclusion of written communication in the concepts of "conversation" and "dialogue." Take "conversation," for instance. This term is repeatedly used to reference oral communication in peer review and related activities, and secondarily used to reference written communication. Bruffee's treatment of writing as "displaced conversation" illustrates the hierarchy related to this term. As we examine Bruffee's explanation again, we see that he does not exactly equate writing with conversation, and supports the primacy of oral communication:

> Like thought, writing is related to conversation in both time and function. [. . .] But because thought is already one step away from conversation, the position of writing relative to conversation is more complex than the position of thought relative to conversation. Writing is at once two steps away from conversation and a return to conversation; we internalize conversation as thought; and then by writing, we re-immerse conversation in its external, social medium. ("Collaboration" 641)

Bruffee seems to be arguing that writing is distant and separate from conversation. Bruffee's description of "peer critiquing" as a written exercise illustrates this point *(A Short Course in Writing)*. Two of the three steps he assigns peer critiquing are written exercises; again, the first step is to objectively describe a student's paper and the second step is to evaluate the student's paper. These steps are written exercises, and Bruffee does not describe them in terms of conversation. Rather, he describes these steps in terms of audience and critical thinking. Only the third step, which he suggests is a *discussion* with the author about the content (ideas) of the paper, is described in terms of conversation.

To further illustrate a separation of speech and writing in peer review, we could reconsider accounts of written discourse by peer review scholars. Marginal comments or completed worksheets for peer review have traditionally not been described as conversation in peer review. Rather, they have been described as supplements or ways to record suggestions (Hawkins 29; Spear, *Sharing Writing*, 101). Clearly, peer review scholars do not eschew writing as a part of peer review activity. What they seemingly advocate, however, is a *separation* of writing and speech. While students may write comments on one another's papers, it is the speech situation that truly defines the activity as social. What happens when writing is no longer secondary, but primary, as in the activity of virtual peer review? What happens when conversations truly become written, as they do on the Internet?

This separation raises the question of whether or not written conversations—displaced conversations—have the same value as speech-based conversations in peer review. The question brings us back to an age-old debate over the supremacy of oral communication articulated by Plato in the *Phaedrus*. In the *Phaedrus*, Socrates argues that writing is inferior to oral communication, for writing weakens the memory and has only the appearance of wisdom

(140). Socrates suggests that writing "has no power to protect or help itself"—that is, no power to respond. Written words, says Socrates, "cannot defend themselves by argument and cannot teach the truth effectually" (141). Since the pursuit of truth is the highest calling for Socrates, he eschews writing as a "bastard" of speech (141), and suggests that writing falsely promises wisdom when it really erodes memory. Clearly, Plato advocates oral communication over written communication. The matter has been taken up by several scholars since then, perhaps most radically by Jacques Derrida, who deconstructs the binaries of speech/writing that Plato outlines (Haas 8). According to Patricia Bizzell and Bruce Herzberg, Derrida reverses Plato's argument, suggesting that "writing is prior to speech—not historically, of course, but conceptually, in that writing shows more clearly than speech does how language is different from what it supposedly represents" (Bizzell and Herzberg 1166). Through deconstruction, Derrida is interested in dissolving binary characterizations of writing and speech altogether.

The debate articulated by Plato and Derrida illuminates the problem of conversation as it applies to written communication and, more specifically, virtual peer review. Because virtual peer review interaction is written, we are squarely confronted with our attitudes and preferences about written communication. In response, I argue that virtual peer review does not rely on the distinctions of speech and writing that were so carefully built in terms of traditional peer review. In other words, virtual peer review resists the primary reference of "conversation" or "dialogue" to oral communication, and instead embraces these terms with a broader understanding. We may find more help from scholars such as Christina Haas, who articulates an extension of Vygotsky's work to address the materiality of writing, and Kay Halasek, who suggests a broad concept of dialogue as it applies to composition instruction. In *Writing Technology: Studies on the Materiality of Literacy*, Haas advocates Vygotsky's social theory of language in support of writing as a technology. Further, she suggests that writing and speech need not be mutually exclusive (13). Using Vygotsky's concept of mediation, Haas explains that Vygotsky was interested in the influence of symbols on human thinking: "Vygotsky brilliantly extended the concept of tool use to include sign systems, including writing, and he referred to such sign systems metaphorically as 'psychological tools'" (14). Haas suggests that, as a psychological tool, "writing mediates my interaction with the social world—and is the means of transformation not only of others (when I persuade through my writing) but also of myself (when I learn from it)" (16). This idea of mediation may be applied to virtual environments—particularly written environments such as those that support virtual peer review. Writing would then be more than a text. It would be a form of expression and, in Haas's word, a "transformation." Curtis Bonk and Donald Cunningham also employ Vygotsky to support electronic discourse, suggesting that computer technology paves the way for new forms of dialogue (35). Taking the view that all language is social, these authors imply that electronic dialogues are compatible with Vygotsky's theory of language development. Like Haas, Bonk and Cunningham have an inclusive view of dialogue that does not distinguish between spoken or written discourse.

Kay Halasek also offers a broader interpretation of dialogue—specifically, Bakhtin's theory of dialogue—that could apply to virtual peer review. Halasek, too, avoids clean distinctions between speech and writing, endorsing instead an overall approach to dialogue, which she describes as a "defining metaphor for the discipline [of composition]" (3–4). She advocates dialogue as "a complex network of statement, response, and restatement, one that, among other things, complicates our understanding of audience and acknowledges the inherent 'addressivity' of all discourse" (6). Halasek also acknowledges both written and spoken discourses as they specifically relate to composition instruction, referring generally to peer review in terms of the "cooperative sharing of texts" (4) and the "actual cooperative verbal exchange between two speaking subjects" (5) as examples of dialogic pedagogy. However, Halasek insists that dialogue reach beyond classroom practices: "[D]ialogism is not restricted to interindividual discussion or sharing of texts, for at the most elemental level of Bakhtinian sociological linguistics lies dialogism. Every word has its own internal dialogism" (6). Clearly, Halasek embraces a broader interpretation of dialogue that goes beyond any practical application—either spoken or written. Her all-encompassing view of dialogism would most assuredly apply to virtual environments as well, because she does not discriminate among any particular practices. Indeed, Halasek suggests a reconceptualization of writing instruction so that it is not just based on dialogic activities for the classroom but on the idea of exchange (cultural as well as linguistic) among students and teachers.

In reviewing these perspectives to illustrate abnormal discourse of virtual peer review, I do not suggest that the ideas forwarded by Halasek or Haas represent abnormal discourse in themselves. Their views may in fact be quite sensible, and even be widely accepted. The point is that peer review literature has not been updated to accommodate these broader perspectives; peer review literature, instead, seems to have referenced "dialogue" and "conversation" specifically in terms of oral communication rather than in terms of these more inclusive perspectives. As we explore peer review in virtual environments, we must acknowledge how written communication resembles dialogue and conversation as well. In the next section I explain how abnormal discourse of virtual peer review manifests in practice.

Abnormal Discourse in Virtual Peer Review Practice

In contrast to the normal discourse of peer review, which I have characterized as the primacy of speech and a separation of speech from writing, virtual peer review places the activity entirely in the realm of writing and thus challenges our perception of speech and written discourses. As Michael Martindale suggests, text-based communication facilitated by computers challenges our ideas of open discourse schemas—those that encourage feedback and response—which have been traditionally assigned to speech situations (109). But research about computer-mediated communication has countered this separation, suggesting that computer-mediated communication can also facilitate interaction, response, and feedback; it just may look different than it looks in speech (Bonk and King; Churchill, Snowdon, and Munro). Not only may online discourse look different, but it may also have different consequences for peer review. For instance, Mark Mabrito found that highly apprehensive students offered more directive comments online than they did face-to-face—a contrast to the "nondirective" code of peer review in writing center tutorials. In addition, Mabrito found that students tended to use directive comments from online peer reviewers more often in their revisions ("Electronic Mail"; see also Rushton, Ramsey, and Rada; Hewett).

Indeed, virtual peer review resembles something quite different than what we have come to identify as speech-based peer review. The handful of scholars who have investigated differences between virtual peer review and face-to-face peer review seem to agree. For example, Beth Hewett suggests in an empirical comparison of face-to-face and online peer review that online "talk" (including both synchronous and asynchronous technologies) seems to resemble a "hybrid" of oral and written communication.

> Like oral language, the CMC talk attempted to be dialogic, to connect with the utterances of others, and to engage them in the open-endedness of oral talk. But, characteristic of written language, it tended to be closed and finite, as when [a student] attempted and failed to reengage the discussion after the group had moved on. CMC is also like oral language in its context dependency. (275–76)

Virtual environments have been described as hybrid by others as well. Eric Crump, for example, suggests that moving activities like peer review to virtual environments "is actually a leap into a new dimension" (178). In discussing the potential of MUDs for conducting writing conferences, Crump acknowledges the similarities and differences the medium has with oral communication, noting that it is more than "just talking": "We're 'just talking' in writing, though. Natural oral fluency, usually ephemeral, is now capturable" (183). He also suggests how MUDs change our thinking about writing: "As writing begins to assume the shape of new technologies, dialogic forms will begin to displace monologic forms that thrived in print" (190). Crump sees the "new dimension" that online discourse affords as an area of exciting and future growth for writing instruction. Mike Palmquist notes also that moving instructional activities online can transform and shape discourse in the class-room; he suggests that online discourse is something other than what we experience in the traditional classroom (see also Sirc and Reynolds).

As we move into this new dimension, however, we must be careful not to fall back into the normal discourse of peer review. Having been encultur-ated by the normal discourse, we may not have the proper terms to identify the practical differences that exist in virtual peer review. We may instead try to use words with which we are familiar—like "talk"—to describe the activ-ity of virtual peer review. As I just discussed, Crump uses "talk" to describe the "oralish" nature of MUDs, while Hewett uses the term in her analysis of face-to-face and online "talk" in peer review. Both scholars, however, illus-trate the struggle that results from using this term. Crump struggles to define the new dimension as something more than talk, while Hewett concludes throughout her study that online "talk" is definitely not the same as talk in face-to-face environments. In fact, Hewett concludes, in accordance with Marshall McLuhan, that the "medium is the message" and that the environ-ments make a big difference in how "talk" plays out in peer response. Hewett suggests that context in virtual environments is not as shared as in speech environments, and that activities such as invention are not as effective in vir-tual environments as they are in oral ones. She does suggest that for the activ-ity of responding directly to student texts, virtual "talk" seems equally as use-ful as face-to-face talk. Nevertheless, Hewett seems to conclude that there is an incompatibility between our understanding of "talk" when it is applied in face-to-face environments and our understanding of it when it is applied to virtual environments.

I concur, and suggest that the word "talk" may not be an appropriate term to describe what happens in virtual peer review, because it is too attached to the normal discourse. Unlike the words "conversation" and "dia-logue," which can be interpreted more broadly to mean the *exchange* of writ-ten as well as spoken discourse, the word "talk" has an immediate connota-tion of oral communication. When we try to apply this term to written communication, we may be, consciously or not, falling back into the normal discourse of oral communication. This slippage begins to translate, I believe, into suggestions that "something is lost" rather than gained when we explore the new dimension of online discourse in virtual peer review. To illustrate, in "If It Ain't Broke Why Fix It?" Irvin Peckham suggests that moving peer review to virtual environments results in "disruption" of a traditional class-room; he describes what is "lost and gained" when moving peer review to vir-tual environments. He ultimately concludes that instructors should consider such a move with great caution, or at least blend online peer review with tra-ditional peer review practices. While Peckham's discussion is valuable in con-sidering moves of peer review to virtual environments, it ultimately endorses the normal discourse by holding oral communication as the norm for peer review, suggesting that virtual peer review doesn't quite match peer review in face-to-face environments.

The tension we feel, then, concerning virtual peer review practice circles around a decision point: we must decide whether or not we want to use the same terms to describe virtual peer review *practice* that we have been using to describe face-to-face peer review practice. The point brings us back to Rorty's notion of abnormal discourse, for he mentions that the vocabulary of normal discourse is well established, but when anomalies occur, we do not have the proper terms to describe them. I argue the same thing is happening as we describe a shift of peer review to virtual environments; we may try to describe the activity in terms of face-to-face practice, but such terms, we are finding, are inappropriate to fully embrace peer review in virtual environments. We come up short almost every time. So while theoretically the concepts of conversation and dialogue broadly conceived accommodate virtual peer review, from a practical standpoint, virtual peer review must be described differently. We must acknowledge that virtual peer review takes us into new territory that we don't quite know yet how to describe.

To better understand the "new dimension" that virtual peer review affords, I suggest that we might find helpful insight by examining issues related to literacy. For example, in trying to describe the communication dimension of virtual peer review, which does not quite fit into the normal discourse of oral communication, we might consider how virtual peer review reflects what Walter Ong calls a "secondary orality." In *Orality and Literacy*, Ong suggests that secondary orality reflects characteristics of orality, but that it is "based permanently on the use of writing and print" (136). Ong appears to be referencing media such as radio and television in his use of secondary orality, but the concept could be applied to Internet communication as well. In *Cyberliteracy: Navigating the Internet with Awareness*, Laura Gurak argues exactly that: secondary orality is appropriate to describe literacy that involves the Internet. Gurak suggests that e-mail in particular has characteristics of oral communication and print communication, but does not quite fit into either category neatly. She suggests that "cyberliteracy is not purely a print literacy, not is it purely an oral literacy. It is an electronic literacy—newly emerging in a new medium—that combines features of both print and the spoken word, and it does so in ways that change how we read, speak, think, and interact with others" (14). Gurak further argues that because of this difference, we must think critically about our communication via the Internet. Considering Gurak's argument in relation to virtual peer review, I agree that peer review requires a new way of thinking of how we respond to one another about writing. It requires us to move away from a firm dichotomy of speech and writing, and to embrace a broader understanding of online communication that involves reading, writing, and interacting. To further flesh out this perspective—this new dimension of virtual peer review practice—I turn to another perspective of literacy that discusses the intersubjectivity of reading and writing as literacy practices.

Specifically, I endorse the view of written communication as a "literacy of involvement"—a phrase that well describes the social interaction that occurs in virtual peer review. In *Literacy as Involvement,* Deborah Brandt depicts written communication in terms of contextual, human activities of reading and writing. Brandt acknowledges the differences of time and space in written communication, but she rejects the idea that distancing of time and space also means the removal of intersubjectivity in the acts of writing and reading (31). Reviewing the work of Jack Goody, Walter Ong, Deborah Tannen, and David Olson, Brandt argues against what she calls "strong-text literacies" that draw sharp distinctions between literacy and orality. Strong-text literacies, according to Brandt, "maintain the classic underlying categories of the oral-like and the literate-like" (19). She suggests that both Goody and Ong, for example, depict writings as artifacts rather than activities (22); she argues that Tannen and Olson "focus on the surface features of finished pieces of discourse as a basis for characterizing literacy" (22). At the heart of Brandt's critique of strong-text literacies is her objection to the depiction of writing as a mere product—something distant, abstract, and removed from context. According to her, strong-text literacies are (1) autonomous, (2) anonymous, and (3) textual. By saying these are autonomous, she means that written language gains power because it "exists, as inscription, independently from the physical presence and even living existence of its author" (23). This characteristic of strong-text literacy suggests a detachment of text from author, or even from the context in which a text was written. Anonymity, she suggests, may diminish our sense of author and reader as persons and instead emphasize texts as things. "Anonymous written language rises as a kind of wall between writer and reader, a third presence that does not exist in talk. As a result, we are said to deal not directly with each other in literate exchanges but deal, on one side or the other, with language. Alignment of consciousness in writing and reading is not with the other but with the language on the page" (24). In regard to textuality, Brandt suggests that written language is separated from physical and temporal dimensions, separated from context and made an object—ossified, in a sense (25).

These characteristics of strong-text literacies, I believe, reflect some of the objections writing instructors may have about moving course activities to virtual environments, and to peer review specifically. Recall Harris's and Russell's strong objections to moving writing center tutoring to virtual environments. They suggested that peer tutoring in virtual environments is "cold" and less "human" than face-to-face tutoring. Brandt's explanations of strong-text literacy make sense of these objections. Of particular relevance, I believe, are the characteristics of autonomy and textuality. Brandt suggests that written language becomes autonomous, in a sense deferring interaction from people to pages. Such an observation resonates with the criticism that online tutoring is less human than face-to-face tutoring, and that interactions occur with writing rather than with people. In addition, the characteristic of textuality suggests a removal from the human element; again, people are taken to deal with texts and not people when communicating through written language. Brandt's depiction of strong-text literacies, in short, may represent our attitudes (and objections) about moving peer review and similar activities out of the face-to-face environment. In accordance with Brandt, I suggest that this view of literacy does not account for our activities as writers and readers. Consider Brandt's argument in response to strong-text literacies, keeping in mind the normal and abnormal discourse I have outlined with regard to virtual peer review:

> [M]y aim is to argue that this whole framework—a framework that puts the literate in tension with the oral, the message in tension with involvement, and the text in tension with context—is the wrong framework for thinking about reading and writing and the nature of literacy. Strong-text models may account at some level for the potential of literacy—that is, they may account for what writing makes possible as a technology that oral language does not. But that is not the same thing as establishing what makes possible the human acts of writing and reading. (Brandt 28)

Rather than considering reading and writing as separate, distant, and unresponsive, Brandt characterizes reading and writing as the "here-and-now," meaning that reading and writing require our constant, present attention for what actions we must take next (99). She blurs differences of time and space by suggesting that writing and reading "are the means by which present-tense literate acts are carried out" (99). Her depiction of literacy as involvement can thus be summarized:

> Moving from the oral to the literate thus does not require embracing a different interpretation of language, context, and meaning [. . .] textual language is always embedded in working contexts of action, driven by the "aim of pursuit," its meaning accessible only in reference to the intersubjective enterprises of those who are involved here. Social involvement is at the center both of our collective literate practices and our seemingly solitary efforts at reading and writing. (Brandt 125)

I believe these arguments about literacy point us in the direction of a reconceptualization of virtual peer review practice—what I am calling abnormal discourse. The normal discourse of peer review, I contend, depicted the primacy of oral communication in terms of providing a context for peer review that was responsive. In the normal discourse, our understandings of conversation and dialogue were first attached to oral communication. Theorizing these terms more broadly helps us accommodate written communication, but may not account for pointed differences of practice. The literacy perspectives I have just reviewed provide a more concrete perspective of practice that relates to virtual peer review, for they dissolve the hierarchies between speech and writing that may have formed the basis of normal discourse. Despite the differences of time, space, and interaction of written communication, these differences do not suggest that written communication is any *less* useful. As Brandt reminds us, writing and reading are just as active and contextual as speaking. Brandt helps us to view written communication—the basis of virtual peer review—as a literacy of involvement rather than a literacy of separateness. Likewise, Gurak suggests that we are not able to pigeonhole Internet communication into firm categories of speech or print; it is something else, something new. When we attempt to fit this newness into the grooves of our normal discourse, we are conflicted.

To embrace the abnormal discourse of virtual peer review practice, then, peer review scholars must acknowledge an extension of the concepts of conversation and dialogue to include written communication. In addition, as we consider peer review as an online activity, we should embrace an understanding of online discourse as a literacy of involvement rather than as a literacy of separateness. As peer review continues to be practiced online with more frequency, these concepts will become critical in further research about virtual peer review. Yet, in practice, we may struggle to fully embrace virtual peer review, because the normal discourse of peer review as an exercise of oral communication has been so strong. Thus, challenges will inevitably surface when we begin to embrace the abnormal discourse of virtual peer review. However, consistent with Rorty's definition of the term, I do not perceive "abnormal discourse" as a negative label in this case. Rather, as abnormal discourse, virtual peer review pushes the boundaries of peer review and opens up new territories of writing practices and instruction. In the next chapter, I explore this new ground using concrete examples of virtual peer review to illustrate the challenges that may arise as we implement virtual peer review.

CHAPTER 4

Challenges of Virtual Peer Review

As I suggested in chapter 3, virtual peer review has marks of "abnormal discourse" because it requires a new way of thinking about peer review. I described this new way of thinking in terms of a "literacy of involvement," or actively reading, writing, and interacting in virtual environments. This depiction of *involvement* and *activity* in virtual environments has not been accounted for in past literature that has emphasized peer review as an exercise of oral communication. In this chapter I further explore how this new way of thinking about peer review might manifest in context. Specifically, I suggest that reading, writing, and interacting are helpful starting points in characterizing the activities involved in virtual peer review. However, these activities in virtual peer review are made more complex by the influence of two additional factors: collaboration and technology. These factors present unique challenges, such as complexities of ownership, authorship, and technological adaptability, that may not be as apparent in face-to-face peer review. If we are to truly embrace virtual peer review in all its "abnormality," we must address these challenges so we are better equipped to conduct virtual peer review. In the following sections, I identify these challenges of collaboration and technology, and I illustrate them through excerpts of actual virtual peer review dialogue.

Challenges Related to Collaboration: Ownership and Authorship

Virtual peer review can be categorized as a collaborative activity in that it involves two or more persons working toward a goal of improving writing, and in this sense, virtual peer review shares roots with peer review as a collaborative activity. As I discussed in chapter 1, peer review has been deeply connected to collaboration both in practice and theory. Scholars have described peer review as collaborative because the activity involves two or more persons conversing with each other about writing, with the goal of helping one another improve writing (Bruffee, "Collaboration"; Gere; DiPardo and Freedman). Bruffee connected this collaborative nature of peer review more broadly to social constructionist theory, which asserts that knowledge is created through social interaction with others. The deep roots of peer review in terms of collaboration, then, have been well established.

Virtual peer review, however, may require finer distinctions with regard to collaboration, because the textual nature of the activity may raise issues of ownership and authorship. For example, when virtual peer reviewers are writing comments to one another, comments can easily be seen as property—as the textual ownership of ideas. In addition, written comments offered from peers may be too easily integrated into texts, thus potentially changing an individually authored text to a collaboratively authored text. Spigelman concurs, noting that "traditional writing groups are face-to-face encounters" and that "Online writing groups raise new and interesting questions about group dynamics and about issues relating to intellectual property" (16). Because virtual peer review introduces complications related to ownership and authorship, the collaborative nature of virtual peer review appears fundamentally different than the collaborative nature of face-to-face peer review. This difference in collaboration is yet another illustration of the remediation of peer review to virtual environments. Thus, we need to carefully distinguish the connection of virtual peer review and collaboration, keeping in mind the complications that arise due to online media and the textual nature of commentary.

To help distinguish forms of collaboration that apply to virtual peer review, I return to DiPardo and Freedman's categories of collaborative activities: "responding to writing, thinking collaboratively, writing collaboratively, and editing student writing" (120). As I remarked in chapter 1, DiPardo and Freedman have asserted that face-to-face peer review best fits the category of "responding to writing." This distinction of collaboration has served peer review well, for it has helped shape boundaries for the activity. However, *virtual* peer review (and other forms of written peer review, such as handwritten comments on print drafts) may extend into the categories of "writing collaboratively" and "editing" student writing—and perhaps even into the category of "thinking collaboratively." Relying on DiPardo and Freedman's collaborative categories for support, I will address the following forms of collaboration in virtual peer review: (1) responding to writing, (2) editing, and (3) collaborative writing. Using excerpts from actual review sessions, I will illustrate how virtual peer review can sometimes move into these categories, and I will describe the challenges that these moves create.

Responding to Writing

First, it is important to demonstrate how virtual peer review commentary can fit into the category of *responding to writing*—the category of collaboration that DiPardo and Freedman advocate for peer review. Certainly, virtual peer review comments lend themselves well to response, and the added benefit is that the response is documented in print for future reference as the author revises (see figure 9). Response from virtual peer reviewers can vary in terms of length and format. While figure 9 demonstrates a paragraph format written in correspondence style, figure 10 demonstrates a more thorough review that addresses aspects of the student's writing point by point.

Virtual peer review response can also vary in terms of function; for example, response could be classified in terms of praise, suggestions, or criticism. In figure 11, the predominant response is one of praise ("The first few paragraphs are strong"; "Your final sentence is great"), although the reviewer also provides suggestions for improvement ("You may want to 'beef up' the section on funding. Perhaps suggest a way to get funding"). Offering direct suggestions has been described as a characteristic of virtual peer review response in previous research: recall that Mabrito and Hewett both found that when peer review was conducted online, more direct comments were included. Like face-to-face peer review, then, virtual peer review is compatible with the category of responding to writing. Of DiPardo and Freedman's categories of collaboration, responding to writing is least problematic and most clear-cut within virtual peer review. Much more can be said about virtual peer review response; one could elaborate on the differences, for example, between synchronous and asynchronous response. In chapter 5, I provide more detail and suggestions for various forms of response in virtual peer review.

<table>
<tr><td>From:</td><td>@tc.umn,edu></td></tr>
<tr><td>To:</td><td>@tc.umn.edu></td></tr>
<tr><td>Sent:</td><td>Monday, February 28, 2000 5:46 PM</td></tr>
<tr><td>Subject:</td><td>Re: paper</td></tr>
</table>

I read your paper and think you have done a very complete job. I really like points you raise regarding the ferrets. I have two recommendations:

1. You might want to put something in that speaks to the economics involved. You hint at it, but I am thinking some of the numbers discussed in the initial introduction by Steve might make you arguments stronger.

2. You might want to consider combining some of your paragraphs. Some of them seem as though they could go together.

That's all I have. E-mail me if you have any further questions. Hope the orgo test went well today.

Figure 9. "Responding to Writing" in Virtual Peer Review

Author:

Reviewer:

To the reviewer: Comment on the following parts of the assignment:

1. What is the definition of sustainable agriculture offered in the reflective writing? List it here.

    The ideal sustainable agriculture is which the well being of the farm, the farmers, and the livestock is the priority maintained by an integration of sophisticated technology to maximize productivity.

2. How has the writer supported his or her definition (through an example, quotation, readings)? Explain how the writer supported his or her definition.

    There were no quotations or examples from the readings, but the author did support her idea in her introduction and body of the essay. The author first discusses that there are two sides debatable in agriculture which both have their good points. Then, the author discusses how science, naturalists, and technology affect the ecosystem and how all of it should be integrated to accomplish a common goal.

3. Has the writer included credible and relevant sources and citations? If so, list one of the sources used. If not, comment on a good place where a source could be added.

    There were no citations. A good place to place to add a source is in the paragraph explaining how every organism on this planet is interrelated with one another in a direct or indirect way. The source could further show the complicated web how every thing is chained together.

4. What style of documentation is the writer using? Provide an example of the in-text citation style used by the author.

    There was no in-text citation present. I am unsure about the documentation style, but I would guess MLA format.

5. Has the writer used correct grammar, punctuation, and spelling? If not, point out one sentence where some improvement is needed.

    Most of the paper was written pretty well. There was one sentence that needed commas shown in the following: "Technology, on the other hand, believes in controlled environment. There were no serious spelling errors, and punctuation was fine.

6. Is the organization easy to follow (are paragraphs organized logically)? Provide an example of a strong topic sentence.

    The organization was logically explained and not hard to follow. "There are two revolutions in agriculture today, both having their supporters and dissenters".

Figure 10. Variation of Form in Virtual Peer Review Response

The first few paragraphs are strong, especially the introductory paragraph. You may want to explain what COAFES is (or perhaps I am a little ignorant). Your final sentence is great, on how to be "a good neighbor".

You may want to "beef up" the section on funding. Perhaps suggest a way to get the funding. (or if you intent to keep it up to COAFES to find their own resources, then it fits)

The section on how to manage manure is good. I thought your suggestion on keeping only a month supply of manure and selling the rest is good.

Forgive the brevity of my comments, overall I think that with the limited information we were given you did a great job.

Figure 11. Variation of Function in Virtual Peer Review Response

---

Watching PBS' version and Hollywood's version of <u>The Scarlet Letter</u> is like watching two completely different films. M~~The~~ main differences between the two include ~~are~~ (the <u>depiction of characters,</u> ~~way the characters are made out to be~~), the way ~~it~~ <u>both</u> <u>shows</u> ~~ends~~ <u>end-</u>, and the message or theme ~~in which~~ <u>that</u> the endings presents.

Figure 12. Sentence-level Edits in Virtual Peer Review

Editing and Associated Challenges

In addition to fitting into the category of responding to writing, virtual peer review can also expand into the collaborative category of editing. This expansion presents a greater challenge than responding to writing. Consider figure 12, which includes editing suggestions for the author. Examples such as this one illustrate a challenge of virtual peer review in practice: to what extent should virtual peer reviewers edit and/or rephrase the writing of another student?

Virtual peer review exemplifies a sharp contrast with face-to-face peer review in that it embraces editing more openly. In face-to-face peer review, editing or rephrasing comments are less likely to surface, unless reviewers are encouraged to write comments on print drafts as well as discuss drafts in person. As DiPardo and Freedman and other scholars have suggested, face-to-face peer review is an opportunity to discuss on a more global level components such as audience, purpose, organization, and content; local errors or corrections are generally overlooked in such discussions. And in some circles such as peer tutoring, editing student work is thought of as unethical; for example, if a tutor were to edit the errors on a student's paper, the student could simply adopt the corrections as if they were his or her own writing. Editing assistance would contribute to the reputation of writing centers being "fix-it shops" rather than places to come to learn about writing. Writing center scholars have responded by carefully distinguishing tutor activities. For example, as I discussed in chapter 3, tutors in writing centers tend to embrace a nondirective approach in which the tutor listens and converses with a student about writing—sometimes tutors are even discouraged from writing on a student draft at all. These tutor behaviors support the philosophy that Stephen North articulated in "The Idea of a Writing Center"—that writing centers are designed to help writers, not *texts*. The goal of writing centers, according to North, is to help students develop as writers—to work with writers and converse with them about ways to improve. This philosophy is enforced in most writing centers, and it is especially evident in phrases on publication materials such as "we do not proofread or edit your work."

The avoidance of editing in writing center tutorial work is understandable; however, in classroom peer review, where power differentials are less of an issue, editing is more acceptable, and sometimes even encouraged in written peer reviews. For example, Harris outlines goals of peer review as including critical reading and awareness of audience concerns ("Collaboration" 376), and thus does not find activities like editing incompatible with peer review. Of editing, Harris notes that "such peer response alerts writers to more careful proofreading as well as to considerations they need to keep in mind" (372). I tend to agree that editing can play an important part in peer review, and this is especially true in written forms of peer review, where students exchange print drafts and comment on those drafts. In fact, as I discovered in a study of written peer review responses (both handwritten and electronic), editing was the most frequent form of response made in handwritten peer reviews. For example, when peer review is conducted by hand on a print draft, reviewers can use handwritten editing marks and comments between lines of text or in the margins, while still preserving the author's original print text (see figure 13). In virtual peer review, as the example in figure 12 shows, editing can also appear while preserving the original text by using word-processing tools like "track changes." However, editing of this sort in virtual peer review can be problematic for students if they simply accept all edits a peer reviewer has made without carefully reviewing them; in some programs this can occur with the single click of a mouse. This would diminish any learning about the mistakes the author may have made and can lead to appropriation. (I discuss this problem in more detail in the next section.) A technique that avoids this pos-

```
as much as the Vet Med in the processing, with only half as much

waste as the Vet Med.  I have decided to even the odds and have

each department pay for its amount of waste.

    Another idea is reducing the number of animals on campus.

However, we are strongly against this. These animals provide an

excellent resource for education.  In comparison to other

universities, the U of M has a minute animal herd.  Also, if we

lost our animals, we would lose a large part of our COAFES

enrollment to other schools.

    We feel that these recommendations will reduce the amount

of manure, and add profit to the departments without losing the

precious education resource of the animals.
```

Figure 13. Edits in Handwritten Peer Review

sibility is to write comments *about* the errors, as shown in figure 14. Note how the reviewer painstakingly explains the distinction between "it's" and "its." The reviewer points out where the errors were made and how to correct them. This type of "explanatory editing" can actually help students more than marking errors; reviewers take time to explain errors, but the authors have to go back to their text, find the error, and correct it. Explanatory editing can actually enhance virtual peer review and would represent an ideal collaborative interaction, comprised of reviewer explanations and author actions. In this vein, editing can mesh well with the goals of strengthening critical reading and audience awareness so often hailed in terms of peer review. Spigelman agrees, noting that "Peer groups offer student writers a genuine audience that can ask for clarification, point to discursive gaps, find errors, and provide purposes for writing beyond performance and evaluation" (15).

Collaborative Writing and Associated Challenges

Although editing can be handled in ways that minimize appropriation, collaborative writing poses more of a problem in that it refers to the production of a coauthored text. Muriel Harris explains: "[C]ollaborative writing is now identified as writing involving two or more writers working together to produce a joint product" ("Collaboration" 369). The necessity of textual response in virtual peer review increases the possibility that reviewers could generate text that could be integrated into an author's original manuscript, thus changing or

> **Date:** Tue, 04 Apr 2000 22:50:04 -0500
> **From:**
>   **To:**
> **Subject:** Re: Peer Review
>
> This was a very convincing memo. The order of the information flowed very well. The history and information about the costs was good background information. The waste removal comparison costs helped to put the issue into perspective.
>
> There were just a few grammatical errors and one unclear sentence:
>
> In the second paragraph the wrong "it's" was used. The correct one is "its", no apostrophe. This occurred in both the second and last sentence. I think you are thinking of it as possessive, but really you are saying "it is." In the last sentence of the second paragraph "cannot" is one word, not two.
>
> In the third paragraph in the first sentence "its" should be one word again.
>
> The sentence "The options to maintaining . . ." in the fifth paragraph was unclear. I realized what it meant as I read on in the paragraph. Maybe "The option of moving the animals off of the St. Paul Campus is not acceptable" would work here.
>
> Wonderful Work!!!

Figure 14. Explanatory Edits in Virtual Peer Review

> **The message or theme of Hollywood's version was, God is the only person who can decide what sin is. The message or theme in PBS' version was, "secret sin can kill you."** These messages influenced two versions of the Scarlet Letter, especially the ending. The way Hollywood's version ends is entirely different from the way PBS' version ends. As Hester is on the scaffold about to be hung for witchcraft, Dimmesdale goes onto the scaffold and admits to fathering Hester's child, Pearl. Then, while Dimmesdale is about to get hung, the savages start a battle with the puritans.

Figure 15. Substantial Contributions from Virtual Peer Reviewer

expanding the goal of virtual peer review from *response* to *collaborative writing*. Figure 15 demonstrates how a virtual peer reviewer can add text to an author's paper using word-processing tools (underlined portions reflect the reviewer's additions). When reviewers use such tools to rephrase or rewrite text, appropriation is made even easier, because an author can opt to "accept changes" made by the reviewer, and all reviewer comments can be incorporated instantly

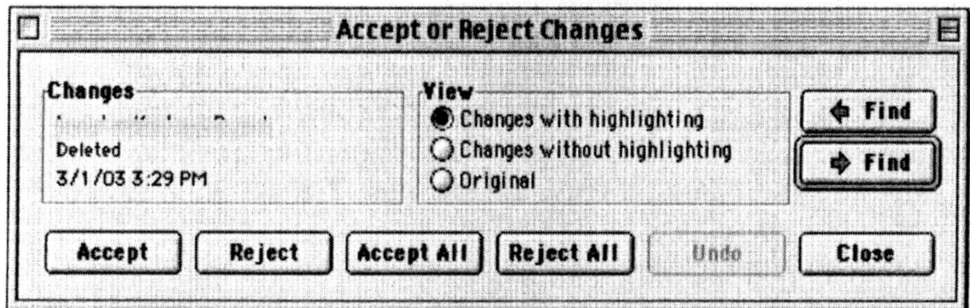

Figure 16. Options for Quickly Accepting Changes in Word Documents

(see figure 16). Thus, these possibilities raise the question: To what degree is collaborative writing present and/or acceptable in virtual peer review? I argue that virtual peer review is a form of collaborative *learning* but should not be a form of collaborative *writing*. The distinction can be made in terms of how we conceive of ownership and authorship—complex issues that must be carefully negotiated in an activity like virtual peer review.

In *Across Property Lines: Textual Ownership in Writing Groups,* Candace Spigelman addresses the issue of peer review and collaborative writing in great detail, focusing on perceptions of textual ownership. She asserts that ownership is a constant tension in peer review groups: "Writing groups illuminate a universal phenomenon: the dialectical tension between the private and public, between writers and readers, for ownership and control of the written text" (23). Spigelman notes that collaboration in peer review can be seen from two theoretical frameworks: expressivism and social constructionism. She suggests that in the expressivist perspective strong notions of ownership exist: "Because the goal of writing is to call forth the profound, personal insights of the writer, unfettered by social influence or interference, the ideas articulated in the expressivist text are very much the property of their author" (129). She says that in contrast, "Social constructionist theories of writing resist the metaphor of private ownership, since texts are always a composite of the social and cultural conditions that construct writers" (118). Spigelman argues that writing groups and peer reviewers endorse *intertextuality,* "the idea that no text is totally original, the private property of an autonomous creator" (17). She invokes Bakhtin to talk about the fluidity of text and utterances, suggesting that texts are always a response to previous utterances and therefore resist individual ownership (17).

Despite her stance that peer review supports intertextuality, or a more fluid perspective of texts, Spigelman says that expressivist perspectives are still a factor in writing groups and peer review work, especially among student writers (20). She explains that students may hold tightly onto notions of individual authorship, inspired by fears of plagiarism and appropriation of texts (21): "Most student writers do think of themselves as textual 'owners' (at least to the extent that they can think of themselves this way, given the competing urgencies of teacher evaluation and appropriation) because they 'know' that writers 'own' their texts" (23). Such fears about plagiarism might influence behavior in writing groups; Spigelman discovered, for example, in her case study of student writers that students carefully monitored their collaborative peer review behaviors:

> [A]lthough the participants employed a discourse of shared ownership as they helped each other to revise, they also imposed unspoken limits on their collaborative engagement: they restricted their comments to matters of addition, clarification, or editing; they accepted only those peers' suggestions which were offered directly or gained by asking permission; they followed a code of ethics that allowed for either an appropriation of ideas but not words or an appropriation of words but not ideas, depending on where they viewed ideas as originating. (127)

The contradiction that Spigelman identifies is fascinating, especially given the social constructionist roots of peer review as a learning activity. It appears that in spite of the social framework in which peer review is placed, students and teachers alike may actually hang on to expressivist views of ownership as they struggle with the possibility that peer review could lead to plagiarism and other improper appropriations of text. Ultimately, Spigelman concludes, writing groups must respond to both individual and collaborative perspectives of textual ownership:

> Perhaps the most important thing we can learn from these writing groups is that the question of ownership is always equivocal. The staunch positions of the expressivists, who claim that students and all writers must believe that they own their texts, is no less accurate than the assertions of social-constructionists, who argue that ownership of writing (of discourse) is impossible. Ultimately, for writing groups to function—and hence for writers to write—they must be committed to both public and private notions of ownership. (132)

While Spigelman's conclusion strikes a nice compromise, I believe virtual peer review requires a sharper distinction in regard to collaborative writing, and this distinction can be made in terms of goals. For example, while Spigelman effectively makes the point that, according to social perspectives, textual ownership is "impossible," there is a difference in goals between co-authored and individually authored texts. Coauthors set out to create a collaborative text, and therefore have much greater freedom with intertextuality than peer reviewers do. Perhaps it is helpful to think of this difference of goals in terms of "collaborative learning" and "collaborative writing," as Muriel Harris does: "Collaborative writing thus refers to products of multiple authors while collaboratively learning about writing involves interaction between writer and reader to help the writer improve her own abilities and produce her own text—though, of course, her final product is influenced by the collaboration with others" ("Collaboration" 370). Interestingly, Harris makes this distinction to separate peer tutoring from peer review, and she suggests that peer review is closer to collaborative writing than peer tutoring is. While this may be true, it is important to reinforce that peer review *is not the same as* collaborative writing, for the goals are different. Going back to figure 15, I would argue that substantial text additions made by the virtual peer reviewer are inappropriate, for they reflect the thoughts of the reviewer instead of the author; this crosses the line from responding to writing to collaborative writing. As I have argued throughout this book, the goal of virtual peer review is to provide response for the purpose of improving writing—not for the purpose of coauthoring a text. This difference is especially important to enforce as peer review moves to virtual environments.

To further illustrate this difference, below I include excerpts of online comments from collaborative groups whose purpose was to create a collaboratively-authored text. These excerpts illustrate that the careful distinctions necessary for peer review dissolve when a group works online for the goal of jointly authoring a text. That is, in collaborative writing groups, *all* categories of collaborative activity highlighted by DiPardo and Freedman occur with fluidity (responding to writing, editing, collaborative writing, and collaborative thinking). In figure 17, for example, students responded to one another on drafts, and also used the online space to produce entire chunks of text that could be copied directly into a collaborative paper. As shown in figure 17, textual commentary facilitated by the Internet can be quite efficient, for group members can comment on other members' contributions, track contributions, and add their own. Figure 18 is another example of how a group member contributes to an overall collaborative project. As shown there, not only are categories of collaborative writing and responding to writing evident, but "collaborative thinking" is evident as well. Collaborative thinking could be defined in many ways, such as brainstorming, problem solving, discussing, forming a consensus, expressing disagreements, or planning how to move a project forward. Figure 19 further illustrates a mix of collaborative thinking—ranging from brainstorming to problem solving to planning. These examples illustrate that when groups set out to write collaboratively, their interactions may encompass several categories of collaborative activities. In contrast, the goal of virtual peer reviewers is primarily to respond to writing and to offer suggestions for improving the document. Thus, collaborative interactions are more limited for virtual peer reviewers than for collaborative writers.

Topic: a very rough draft (1 of 1), Read 5 times
Conf: Group 2 (Mpls)
From: 0003@umn.edu
Date: Sunday, March 19, 2000 10:29 PM

here is a very rough draft. however I have no idea what a press release style is. also I couldn't really prove that it would be economically sound to use the foxes instead of the virus. because I have no idea how much it would cost to intorduce such a population. any ideas?

New Zealand, February 1987,
In the last few decades land degradation in high rabbit population, semiarid areas of New Zealand has been extensive. Therefore, rabbits are regarded as extremely destructive and needing control. One of our options was to control the rabbit population by biocontrol means, namely the introduction of myxomatosis virus. Biocontrol methods are often considered to be more specific for the pest organisms and, thus, safer for the environment Controversy over the introduction of myxomatosis centered mostly on whether the disease was humane and effective means for controlling rabbits. Rabbit control rates have increased 220% in the last three years on our very rabbit-prone country and these increases will have to continue to offset the taxpayer fund reductions.

Because this region has a unique landscape, it must be protected for this and future generations. Unless successful methods are available to control the rabbit then inevitably the landscape and the environment will suffer with ultimate cost to the nation both directly and indirectly. In addition, the majority of the New Zealand public would be particularly upset to find diseased animals, due to the introduction of myxomatosis, on public lands in the course of their recreational pursuits. Also the long term results on population affected by the virus are not guaranteed, because any population that is continuously exposed to the same disease develops a level of resistance because of the wide range of genetic diversity in the population.

Post New Topic | Reply to: "a very rough draft"

Figure 17. Generating Text for Collaborative Writing Assignments

As this discussion demonstrates, important complexities of collaboration surface when we think about peer review moving to virtual environments. Some of these complexities are also present in face-to-face peer review, but issues of ownership and authorship are more urgent in virtual peer review and demand careful and clear distinctions. It is true that online technologies facilitate (quite easily, in fact) all four categories of collaboration: response to writing, editing, collaborative writing, and collaborative thinking. Virtual peer

Topic: info, reply (2 of 3), Read 21 times
Conf: Group 1
From: 0012@umn.edu
Date: Sunday, February 20, 2000 05:14 PM

Hi guys, am I doing this right? Anyway, I came up with some things. I like ______'s definition (especially the source) I put in my vote to use that.

Here is my list of environmental rewards and risks.
Rewards:
* reduced reliance on chemical pesticides
* increased crop yield
* preservation of biodiversity through needing to use less and getting more
Risks:
*uncontrolled dispersal of modified organisms
*legal patents may restrict use and reward the few who gain to profit from technology
*difficulty in regulation (laws can't keep up with changes in technology)

I have chosen a couple of good quotes from the reading, and plan on researching a good choice for question #3, a genetically engineered organism.

Who wants to compose the draft of this paper? I would be happy to, if that is OK (or if someone else has their heart set on typing this paper, that is cool too) I will get back to let you know what I find on an organism. (This is the kind of stuff I read for fun, so I am going to the bookstore to see what I can find)

Figure 18. Variety of Collaborative Activities in Collaborative Writing Project

Topic: Reply (3 of 3), Read 15 times
Conf: Group 1 (Mpls)
From: 0044@umn.edu
Date: Sunday, February 20, 2000 08:45 PM

, I am totally ok with you writing this. If at any point you want help or a question answered, my number is   . I also check my e-mail rather frequently, especially in the evening. I am good for calls until 12 always and you can try E-mail later if you need to.

As for question 2, I think you guys touched on all of the main points...it's really just a matter of writing them in sentences. I think the basic point is to be sure the following three points are exemplified:

ethics
economics
ecological/environmental factors

The only one that I think might have gotten left out, and maybe it wasn't and i am remembering wrong, is economics. The third column on page 610 and first on 611 cover this.

Let me/us know what you find out for question three. If you find something that you think will work well, go with it. Otherwise we could possibly use the bovine growth hormone. I think that one point that could be worked in with any choice is that we don't know many of the detriments due to lack of testing and long-term observation of impacts upon organ-isms. We really are going quite blindly into this field. This also could be used in question 2.

Figure 19. Collaborative Thinking in Asynchronous Group Conference

review, however, can be distinguished from other online collaborative activities by examining its goal: to provide response for the purpose of improving writing. The key, then, is to identify the goals of various collaborative activities. As I discuss in chapter 5, goals must always lead actions that are completed online. Problems arise, I believe, when virtual peer reviewers are not aware of the importance of goals and neglect to establish them in their online groups. I will revisit the issue of setting goals for virtual peer review in chapter 5. In the next section, however, I address another set of challenges that surface with virtual peer review: challenges of the technological sort.

Challenges Related to Technology

In addition to challenges related to collaboration, virtual peer review includes challenges associated with technology. These include (1) selecting technology appropriate to the activity, (2) discovering the "frustration factor" or ease of use (usability—access and compatibility), and (3) identifying attitudes about technology that negatively impact a writer's use of the technology. Once again, each of these challenges exemplifies how virtual peer review is a remediation of peer review, for these challenges are not present in the face-to-face form of peer review; nor are they present in written forms of peer review such as handwritten peer review, for virtual peer review relies solely on computer technology for composing, exchanging drafts, and responding to writing. Yet each of these challenges can powerfully impact the experience of virtual peer reviewers, for ill or for good.

Selecting Technology Appropriate to the Activity

On the surface, it might seem that selecting technology for virtual peer review is not a challenge but just simply a decision that has to be made. However, there is a dizzying array of programs that could be used for virtual peer review. Here I discuss factors that make selecting appropriate technology a challenge.

The search for technology that appropriately accommodates virtual peer review leads, in most cases, to what is known as "collaborative technologies." Why, given the previous discussion about the complexities of collaboration and virtual peer review, would the search lead to *collaborative* technologies? To begin, technologies labeled "collaborative" generally facilitate interaction between two or more persons. Virtual peer review certainly fits into this general category, even though it has specific distinctions with regard to collaboration.

The range of collaborative technologies is impressive, though some are better known than others. A common term associated with collaborative technologies is "groupware," or "software that supports groups of people engaged in a common task (or goal) and provides an interface to a shared environment" (Honeycutt and Ferarro, qtd. in Burnett and Clark 173). Although the term "groupware" surfaces quite often in this generic way (see Forman), it is not necessarily an umbrella term and does not represent all collaborative technologies. For example, Lee Honeycutt and Anne Ferraro name "groupware" as only one collaborative technology amidst others such as computer conferencing, bulletin boards/Usenets, desktop conferencing, distance learning, Distributed Computing Environment (DCE), e-mail, Internet Relay Chat (IRC), listservs, MOOs, MUDs, teamware, teleconferencing, workflow, and World Wide Web (qtd. in Burnett and Clark 173). This list would be multiplied if it included names of specific collaborative software programs; such programs change so rapidly, however, that a comprehensive list would always be outdated. The point is that the range of collaborative technologies is truly overwhelming.

How does one begin to sort through these options to select a technology appropriate for virtual peer review? In a discussion of electronic collaboration, Rebecca Burnett and David Clark suggest four factors to address when considering collaborative technologies: (1) *group characteristics,* such as the size of the group, proximity (distance), and other demographics; (2) *group agreements,* such as decisions that the group has made about their collaborative processes; (3) *task characteristics,* pertaining to the goal of the collaborative interaction; and (4) *technology environment,* such as the characteristics and accessibility of the technology (178). These factors can help sort through the complexities associated with electronic collaboration. They note: "Collaboration itself is difficult, and it is further complicated because tasks appropriate for collaboration are usually complex and ill defined" (175). The four factors they identify help match the aims and goals of various collaborative activities with collaborative technologies.

When applied to virtual peer review, these factors can be quite helpful in selecting software programs. In table 3, I show how these factors can influence decisions about technology for virtual peer review. The right-hand column, "Range for Virtual Peer Review," shows options for how virtual peer review could be configured. As this table demonstrates, the four factors of group characteristics, group agreements, task characteristics, and technology environment help to flesh out the range of possibilities for conducting virtual peer review; these distinctions can then lead to more specific decisions about technology selection. In addition, this table reminds us to consider the group and task *before* considering technology. Such steps are imperative for technology selection; it is when we fail to consider these factors that we allow technology to dictate our tasks and goals. Note that among the four factors Burnett and Clark mention, technology is last, reinforcing the idea that goals must precede technology. In chapter 1, I mentioned that in pedagogical contexts, scholars have advocated that pedagogy drive technology and not the other way around. In chapter 5, I again return to this concept by suggesting that our goals for using technology drive our choices.

With decisions in hand about group characteristics, group agreements, task characteristics, and technology environment, selecting technologies becomes much easier. It is only at this point—when all other decisions have been made about the group and task—that one should consider looking at features of individual programs. Consider the following scenarios:

Two students would like to conduct a virtual peer review of one another's assignments for a writing class. They would like to complete the assignment using delayed interactions, and they have set a deadline of two days to complete the virtual peer review. Their teacher has requested that they provide intertextual notes and endnotes, and that they submit their peer-reviewed documents to her electronically using a word-processing program. Given these decisions, the students decided to use e-mail with Word document attachments. The word-processing programs they were using allowed them to enter intertextual comments that were a different color, plus they could add comments at the end of the document. They saved the virtual peer reviews they received and turned them into their teacher with a final draft.

A writing center director would like tutors to work with students online in thirty-minute sessions. The director wants the tutorials to be as similar to face-to-face discussions as possible and does not want tutors to write directly on student texts. Rather, the director wants tutorials to reflect discussion about the writing. The director selects NetMeeting, a conferencing program that allows tutors and students to connect at a specified time. The program has the capability to display a document to separate parties while also facilitating a synchronous chat about the document. From separate computers, tutor and student log in (using passwords provided by the writing center), view the student's document, and have an online discussion about the assignment.

A group of four engineers is assigned to write a report about a project in their firm. Each of the four engineers has written a different section of the report, and one of the engineers is located in a branch firm in another state. A project leader has been chosen from the home site to guide the work to completion. The report is due in two weeks; a rough draft of the report already exists. The group has been told to get feedback on the report from their manager and the legal department before writing the final report. Using a groupware program

Table 3

Factors for Selecting Appropriate Technologies for Virtual Peer Review

Factor of Collaboration	Breakdown of Factor	Range for Virtual Peer Review
Group Characteristics	Size of group	• 1–2 people • 3–4 people • 4–8 people (for larger projects)

	Proximity of group	• Potential for face-to-face review but work mostly likely conducted via distance
		  • Students—across campus or town
		  • Workplace professionals—within office, country, or world

	Demographic characteristics	• Demographics to be determined by the makeup of specific groups
		  • Students
		  • Workplace professionals
		  • Professional writers
		  • Academics
		  • Anyone with computer access

Group Agreements	Decisions about how members of the group will work with each other	• Time frame for completing virtual peer review
		• Synchronous response—real-time chat for group discussion
		• Asynchronous response—delayed interactions for detailed responses
		  • Form of commentary (intertextual notes; end notes; worksheet heuristic)
		  • Function of comments (editing, suggesting, questioning, praising)
		  • Formality of comments (formal or informal sentence structure)

Task Characteristics	Familiarity with task	• Experience of group members in use of electronic technology to discuss or comment on writing • Previous experience with reviewing, but no experience with collaborative technologies

(continued on next page)

Table 3 *(continued)*

Factor of Collaboration	Breakdown of Factor	Range for Virtual Peer Review
		• Previous experience with collaborative technologies, but not with peer review • Previous experience with both peer review and collaborative technologies
	Kinds of documents to be created	• Transcripts of synchronous discussions • Separate word-processing documents with reviewer comments • Original author manuscripts (word processing) with intertextual comments and/or editing

Technology Environment	Characteristics of technology chosen	• Synchronous
		  • Synchronous chat with windows for group and/or private chats
		  • Split screens that accommodate document viewing, synchronous chat, and audio or visual capability
		• Asynchronous
		  • Availability of comments functions
		  • Use of color or highlights for comments
		  • Ability to accept or reject reviewer comments
		  • Placement of comments (margins, intertextual, other)

	Access to technology	• Intranets (only within specified contexts; e.g., workplaces) • Internet (accessible via World Wide Web) • Password-protected sites (need special ID to participate) • Access from only specific computers or from any computer
	Technical support	• Support provided by manufacturers of software • Support provided by person working near group (e.g., instructor; technical support staff in a workplace environment) • No technical support provided

> *that is accessible to their firm, they send the report first to the manager and second to the legal department, asking for feedback in the form of intertextual comments on any details that need to be changed. Edits are welcome. The deadline for returning comments is one week. The manager completes the review, adds comments coded in blue. The engineers then send the document to the legal department. The legal department representative adds comments in green and sends it back to the group. The group leader calls for a synchronous meeting to review the document and discuss proposed changes.*

As these scenarios demonstrate, the groups in these examples had different goals for completing virtual peer review and thus had different technological needs. Decisions based on the group and task characteristics helped them select technologies that fit their unique situations.

Discovering the "Frustration Factor," or Usability

There is no doubt that, even when steps have been taken to make careful decisions about technology selection, unexpected problems with technology may occur—problems such as inaccessibility, lack of technical support, difficulty finding and using functions, or incompatibility across platforms. I call these problems the "frustration factor," or the degree to which the selected technology is easy or difficult to use. A more formal label for the frustration factor is *usability,* or "the question of whether an artifact [. . .] can suitably support its users' tasks" (Spinuzzi 1). An entire body of research exists related to usability, and it spans disciplines such as human factors, ergonomics, psychology, computer science, and technical communication. Recently, much attention has been given to the usability of computer interface designs (Nielsen; Redish; Hackos and Redish), and this focus makes usability especially relevant to activities such as virtual peer review. A brief background about usability might help the reader understand how usability can address the frustration factor in activities like virtual peer review.

Usability can generally be described as having two emphases: design and evaluation. Most usability scholars interested in design focus on *user-centered design* (UCD), a design approach that integrates perspectives from designers, systems, and users simultaneously (MacKenzie). The goal of most UCD designers is to develop a product or document that is self-explanatory and requires the least amount of effort from a user. The other emphasis of usability is *evaluation,* or methods to examine existing designs for potential problems or flaws. The goal of evaluation is to uncover problems so that designers can then address the problems in the next version of the product. I will address here issues of usability *evaluation,* since in this discussion I am concerned with how virtual peer reviewers are *using* applications rather than designing them.

In the following paragraphs I will also try to show how usability evaluation can inform the "frustration factor" we may experience in virtual peer review.

Usability evaluation is conducted using a variety of methods to uncover various usability problems. A popular method of evaluation is *usability testing*, in which researchers observe representative users completing a specified task and locate the problems that users encounter (J. Rubin; Dumas and Redish). Depending on how many users are observed during testing, results of usability testing can reveal up to 90 percent of usability problems (Virzi). After discovering usability problems, researchers can then review the problems and rank them in order of severity. In the *Handbook of Usability Testing*, Jeffrey Rubin shares a "Problem Severity Ranking" that consists of four categories: unusable, severe, moderate, and irritant (278). The *unusable* ranking indicates that a problem completely stops the user from finishing a task—a computer crashing would be an example of something deserving an *unusable* ranking. A *severe* ranking indicates that the user can complete a task, but only with great difficulty, and will be unlikely to use the product again. A *moderate* ranking indicates that a task can be completed, but with *moderate* effort. An *irritant* ranking indicates that the problem does not cause any major difficulties and can be avoided by taking other steps (278).

These rankings of severity can help clarify the types of usability problems that surface—and unfortunately, problems most likely will with surface with any technology. The question becomes one of severity: How severe is the problem that occurs, and does it drastically impede the completion of the task? In virtual peer review, the most severe problems that could occur are ones related to inaccessibility. By "inaccessibility" I mean the inability of virtual peer reviewers to access either a system or a program for any of the following reasons: the users do not have access to the Internet; the users have limited or very slow access to Internet; their computer does not have enough memory to facilitate the downloading and uploading of documents; the users do not have passwords or necessary codes to access a program; the software program crashes due to overuse and lack of power. Problems of inaccessibility are severe, because they may inhibit or discourage users from completing a task altogether. In the case of slow Internet service, for example, some usability research has shown that users get impatient if they experience a delay of even a few seconds (Spool et al.). Given a slow Internet connection, in virtual peer review uploading or downloading documents may take up to five minutes—a very discouraging prospect for users who expect immediacy through the Internet. Problems of inaccessibility are perhaps the most severe usability problems that could occur—bordering on Rubin's ranking of "unusable." If virtual peer reviewers experience these problems, they could be permanently discouraged from using technology again for peer review. And, typically, problems of this severity need the attention of trained technical support staff. This need could cause an additional obstacle if no support is available, thus further discouraging users from trying virtual peer review.

Incompatibility is also a usability problem that could occur with virtual peer review, although it is not as severe as inaccessibility. Incompatibility refers to the inability of computers to read various documents or software programs. For example, incompatibility is frequently a complaint among people who use both Macintosh and PC computers—sometimes the two platforms do not communicate well with each other. Problems with incompatibility are relevant to virtual peer review, because computer platforms and software can vary enormously among persons conducting virtual peer review. How many times, for example, have you received an attachment via e-mail that you were not able to open? Such is an example of incompatibility. In virtual peer review, incompatibility can cause no end of frustration, particularly if reviewers are operating asynchronously and are on a timeline. Say, for example, that a writer sends his manuscript via e-mail attachment to a reviewer, hoping to receive feedback within three days. The reviewer does not check e-mail for two days, and discovers that she cannot open the document sent by the author. She sends a message back to the author explaining the problem and waits for a reply. By the time the author checks e-mail again, it is the third day—the day he was hoping to receive feedback from the reviewer. The review cycle then becomes delayed.

However annoying incompatibility is, there are ways around this type of usability problem. First, reviewers and authors should discuss what programs and platforms they are using before virtual peer review occurs. This can make easier the exchange of documents online. Sometimes, especially in the case of Macintosh and PC platforms, incompatibility can be resolved. For example, Macintosh computers do not require tags when users save a document; PC computers do, and often tags are automatically assigned (.doc for Microsoft Word documents; .xls for Excel documents; .ppt for PowerPoint, etc.). PC computers also do not permit spaces in document names; nor are certain characters permitted (such as the forward slash [/] in a document name). If Macintosh users rename documents, eliminating spaces and characters, and add a tag, the problem of incompatibility might be solved. In the case that naming documents does not solve the problem, a second option authors can try is to reformat their documents using "Rich Text Format" or RTF. Most word-processing programs allow for the option of saving a document as RTF. Rich text format might strip formatting from a document, but usually text arrives intact. A third solution to the problem of incompatibility requires simple e-mail. If attachments or documents cannot be transferred for whatever reason, authors can copy the entire text of their document and paste it into an e-mail message. This move makes for very long e-mail messages but does not hinder virtual peer review. Problems of incompatibility, then, can be addressed and sometimes solved. Because there are ways around problems of incompatibility, these problems could receive a ranking of "moderate" severity. They do slow down virtual peer review, but can be avoided if authors and reviewers take appropriate steps.

In addition to problems of inaccessibility and incompatibility, other usability problems might occur in virtual peer review, such as difficulty using particular software tools for comment or response in virtual peer review. As I alluded to earlier, several word-processing programs include some kind of "comment" function whereby reviewers can highlight, add, delete, or change text, in some cases while preserving the original text with a "cross out" symbol (~~like this~~). When authors receive documents that incorporate such markings, they may not know how to get rid of the markings so they can work on the final documents. Most software programs don't make this process easy; quite often a user will need to search the program or use online help to figure out how to remove markings. However, once reviewers have gone through this process initially, they are likely to complete this task more quickly as they become familiar with the software functions. Such problems might be categorized as "irritant" on Rubin's severity ranking.

As these examples illustrate, a number of usability problems might occur when conducting virtual peer review. Despite the temptation we may have to simply blame technology, the truth is that usability problems do not occur in a vacuum. Handling these problems depends on a number of factors: the severity of the problem, the patience of the user, and the knowledge the user has about troubleshooting such problems. As Clay Spinuzzi suggests, usability is not a problem of technology but one of activity systems—how users interact with technology in larger contexts. Spinuzzi suggests that usability is not "located" in artifacts but rather in the intricate ways in which people use them, and how larger contexts (institutional or workplace, for example) govern those artifacts. Considering the larger contextual picture, it is almost impossible to predict all usability problems that may surface in any given task. However, identifying our individual practices and communicating those practices to fellow collaborators goes a long way toward reducing the frustration factor.

Identifying Negative Attitudes about Technology

The final category of technological challenges related to virtual peer review is one that is perhaps beyond anyone's control: negative attitudes about technology. As I discussed in earlier chapters, there might be several reasons that people have negative attitudes: they have gotten along without technology for years and don't find it necessary; they do not find the use of technology their responsibility (especially in the case of instructors who teach in traditional classrooms); or they have had bad experiences with technology and find it more frustrating than useful. Attitudes about technology can vary widely. Negative attitudes about technology can greatly impede the activity of virtual peer review. For example, persons with negative attitudes about technology might simply avoid virtual peer review or resort to other forms of peer review, such as printing the document, writing comments by hand, and mailing their comments to the reviewer. Although these other forms of peer review are certainly just as useful, they might disrupt peer review practices that the author had expected, and such disruptions might delay peer review.

Negative attitudes about technology might impact virtual peer review the most in instructional contexts, where an instructor might aim to introduce students to methods of virtual peer review. Attitudes can figure in this scenario in a couple of ways. First, instructors might have varying levels of experience and confidence about integrating technology for writing assignments—introducing virtual peer review very well might be unfamiliar territory for them. Second, students likewise bring varying levels of experience and confidence with technology. It is hard to know how these levels might break down for any class, but most often a wide range exists, which is difficult to manage among groups of twenty or more students. In addition, negative attitudes might be influenced by other factors, such as the technology chosen to support virtual peer review. If, for example, the chosen technology has severe usability problems, students might opt to skip the technology altogether and find other methods of peer review; instructors likewise might be tempted to encourage such deviation. An analogy of "footpaths" comes to mind when thinking about this phenomenon—our tendency to choose routes that seem easier and more convenient. For example, the campus where I attended graduate school was fortunate to have a lot of green space with several beautiful lawns. To preserve the green space, many sidewalks were constructed to guide students from building to building. However, sometimes the sidewalks did not follow a direct line from building to building, and footpaths in the grass began to appear that represented more direct routes—and these footpaths became rather permanent. As I walked to school every day, I found myself using the worn footpaths more often than the sidewalks. They simply provided a more direct way to get where I was going.

The same phenomenon might occur in classrooms where virtual peer review is instructed. Although instructors might take very deliberate steps in organizing technologies for students to use (and even include training), students might avoid the technology if enough (or even just a few) problems occur. This occurred in a class I observed. A particular technology was selected for purposes of virtual peer review, but students ignored it and used simple e-mail instead. In fact, in the case of virtual peer review, students often opt for the *lowest common denominator* in technology—that is, technology that they know will be accessible, usable, and require the least amount of effort. In the case I observed, e-mail was the lowest common denominator, and students who used e-mail for virtual peer review were quite happy using it rather than the technology designated for the class. This finding is apparently not uncommon. Bonk and King suggest that among collaborative technologies used for instructional purposes, e-mail seems to be used most widely and frequently (10). When an instructor has gone to great lengths to incorporate a particular technology, moving towards the lowest common denominator can be quite frustrating, perhaps reinforcing negative attitudes about technology. At the same time, it might be more beneficial to simply follow the existing footpaths rather than invest in expensive technology that is unlikely to be used. Decisions one way or the other require careful planning and thought.

The challenges of technology related to virtual peer review—selecting appropriate technology, discovering the frustration factor, and identifying attitudes about technology—all can have an impact on the type of experience writers and reviewers have with virtual peer review. Each of these challenges adds a new layer of complexity, contributing to the seeming "abnormality" of peer review through computer-based activity. As Irvin Peckham observed, when considering whether or not to try virtual peer review it might be easier "[to wait] until more useful technology comes along" (337). Yet this attitude is not useful; it does not help us better understand the virtual forms of peer review, which, as I have suggested, are already here and are likely to occur in our daily lives with more frequency. Moving to virtual peer review requires an awareness of these new layers of complexity, as well as the patience to explore the new territory of collaborative technologies. In the section below, I share a story of a class, mentioned briefly above, in which instructors and students alike struggled to incorporate virtual peer review, and how they confronted specific challenges related to collaboration and technology.

Challenges of Moving toward Virtual Peer Review: A Case in Point

As I have argued throughout this book, the remediation of peer review to virtual environments is one of difference, not similarity. Because of the challenges presented by virtual peer review—challenges that are not present in the face-to-face version of the activity—we cannot expect that transitioning to virtual environments is necessarily intuitive. The story that I share below illustrates how unanticipated challenges related to collaboration and technology can arise when trying to integrate collaborative technologies for peer review and other collaborative writing assignments. Before discussing the challenges that surfaced, I first share background about the course, instructors, and students.

Background. The course, titled "Environment, Global Food Production, and the Citizen," was a combined agronomy and animal science course (two sections of the same course) at a large Midwestern university, and it was classified as writing-intensive. The writing-intensive designation meant that at least ten pages of writing were required and that students needed to complete at least one revision during the semester-long course. In addition to the writing-intensive designation, the course was taught via Interactive Television (ITV); therefore, the two sections were connected via television for every class. Each section of the course included twenty-three students. The students were mostly juniors and seniors in college, and most students were pursuing a bachelor's degree in agriculture. There were two instructors, one for each section of twenty-three students; one instructor was present at each site, and the course functioned through interactive dialogue between instructors and students at both sites.[4]

In this class, students were required to conduct peer review for three individual writing assignments and were assigned peer review partners. Students also were assigned three collaborative writing assignments, for which they worked in groups of three to four students. To help students with writing assignments, the instructors set up access to a collaborative technology called WebBoard to facilitate exchange between students. WebBoard is an online discussion program that allows participants to post documents, post asynchronous messages on a bulletin board, and join synchronous chats. WebBoard also allows these tools to be used within designated group spaces (e.g., instructors can create secure WebBoard group spaces in which groups can use both synchronous and asynchronous tools for their collaborative projects). In addition to WebBoard technology, students were encouraged to use their e-mail accounts for peer review and collaborative projects.

Unanticipated Challenges. The greatest unanticipated challenge that surfaced in this course was the failure of the WebBoard technology. About halfway through the course, the server that housed WebBoard began crashing with regularity. And when WebBoard did function, it functioned slowly. Students began complaining to each other and to instructors that they could not access WebBoard for their collaborative assignments. Only one of the instructors was responsive to these complaints; it was agreed early on that the other instructor would not address technology issues for the class. The instructor handling the technical aspects then contacted a technical support staff person, who was a faculty member at their college; however, this person told them that there was little that could be done to make the server function any better. Thus, no solution was actually provided for the technological problems. As a result, students began relying less and less on WebBoard for their projects.

This unanticipated challenge represented a usability problem of inaccessibility and thus represents the most severe usability category—unusable technology. The slowness of the server and its inability to support WebBoard blocked the use of the technology. This type of problem was beyond the control of the instructors, apparently beyond the control of technical support staff, and certainly beyond the control of students in the course. It caused a real problem. What could have been done to prevent this problem? Obviously, WebBoard was not a good choice for this particular class. Recall the earlier discussion about selection of technology and the many factors that were listed as considerations for collaborative technologies. Perhaps stepping through that decision process more carefully would have helped the situation; however, in reality, instructors do not always have this luxury. In this case, the instructors took the word of the technical support staff that WebBoard was the program they should use. Instructors were limited by both resources and cost— and by what was made immediately available to them. Fortunately, the WebBoard failure occurred when most of the writing assignments had been completed. For remaining writing assignments, instructors simply advised students to use e-mail to communicate with their collaborative partners. This advice illustrates the "lowest common denominator" phenomenon I described earlier. When all else fails, people tend to use what seems to work best and most directly. Although e-mail was less tailored to the specific needs of this course, it allowed students to interact with each other about writing. Thus, e-mail was a viable alternative for the students in this course.

Another unanticipated challenge that arose in this class had to do with the lack of training for all the types of collaborative activities that might occur using technology. As I mentioned earlier, students were asked to complete three peer reviews (in assigned pairs) and three collaborative writing assignments (in assigned groups). To prepare students for these activities, training was provided in two areas: peer review and WebBoard technology. For peer review, students were given specific instructions for critiquing each other's writing, and were given peer review worksheets to guide peer review for each assignment. Peer review instructions included advice for giving constructive feedback and understanding student and author roles. Students were also given handouts with instructions for using the WebBoard technology. These instructions included specific steps for accessing the technology, posting e-mail messages, and replying to other students. A copy of all instructions can be found in appendix C. In addition, students were assigned to one of twelve student groups on the WebBoard. In these groups, students had access to the bulletin board and synchronous chats, and had the ability to post documents to their group. Thus, for collaborative papers, students could choose to use either synchronous or asynchronous technologies that the WebBoard afforded.

Although the training emphasized important aspects of peer review, as well as concrete steps for using the WebBoard technology, training did not address how to use technology *for* peer review. That is, groups were set up in WebBoard to facilitate the collaborative writing assignments, but pairs were not set up in WebBoard to facilitate peer review. This was less the fault of instructors than of a guest speaker who provided the training. It was assumed by the guest speaker that, having instructions for WebBoard, students would make use of the synchronous and asynchronous technologies if they wanted to for virtual peer review. But examples of how to use the technology for virtual peer review were not covered; nor were ways of providing comments online. Consequently, not one student in the course used WebBoard technology for virtual peer review; the majority of students simply conducted peer review by writing on print drafts.

This illustrates how aspects of collaboration can be blurred. Recall the earlier discussion of challenges that occur when we do not distinguish the goals of various collaborative activities such as responding to writing, writing collaboratively, editing, and thinking collaboratively. In this case, the technology was introduced to students, but it was only made clear how the technology would be used for collaborative writing—not for responding to writing through peer review. That only groups were set up on WebBoard suggested that WebBoard was only to be used for collaborative writing. There was an assumption that virtual peer review did not require any different approach and that students would simply use the technologies on WebBoard to facilitate the activity.

Despite this shortcoming, which again was not the fault of the instructors, an interesting thing occurred with regard to peer review in this class. Although WebBoard had not been set up to accommodate peer review, some student pairs began conducting peer review using e-mail. This occurred among approximately 24 percent of the students in this class; the rest of the students conducted peer review through writing on print drafts. While not a majority, the students who used e-mail for peer review used it rather consistently throughout the course to exchange drafts of their papers and provide comments. Had this outcome been anticipated, perhaps instructors would have emphasized more frequently the use of e-mail to conduct peer review in the course. One way this outcome could have been anticipated would have been to find out from students early on about their familiarity with peer review and with technology. A simple survey would have achieved this goal. In this particular course, it was found out after the fact that 98 percent of the class said they were familiar with e-mail; only 9 percent had previous experience using WebBoard. This finding suggests that e-mail may have been a better technology to support virtual peer review than WebBoard for this particular class.

A final unanticipated challenge that arose in this class was the lack of familiarity students had in responding to writing online—in short, the peer reviews that were completed using e-mail were typically shorter and less rich than handwritten peer reviews. For example, handwritten peer reviews reflected a variety of comments ranging from editing to questions to suggestions. In contrast, the most common type of comment found in e-mail peer reviews was that of praise—complimenting the author on something that was well done. Suggestions were also common in e-mail peer reviews, which demonstrated that reviewers were providing substantive comments; however, the frequency of praise in e-mail peer reviews was somewhat surprising. In addition, handwritten peer reviews reflected more variety of form than e-mail peer reviews. For example, handwritten peer reviews included comments written in the margins, between lines of texts, and at the end of a student paper. In contrast, all e-mail peer reviews except one reflected only an end comment—a separate e-mail message written to the student writer. None of the e-mail peer reviews in this case included intertextual comments that made use of word-processing editing or comment functions; as a result, overall e-mail peer reviews tended to focus on global comments and overall suggestions rather than to give local, sentence-level suggestions (thus reflecting less richness). This finding could be explained by the fact that training for the peer review did not include how to use features of word-processing programs to provide intertextual comments.

So, what lessons can be learned from this story? The main lesson of this story is that distinctions between collaboration and technology need to be carefully made from the very beginning. Finding out about background and comfort level with technology would have assisted in the selection of technology. In addition, the ways in which technology would accommodate collaborative assignments needed to be made clearer. In this case, it was assumed that WebBoard would accommodate both collaborative writing assignments and peer review, and that turned out not to be the case. Finally, if technology is to be used for peer review, writers need some orientation to the capabilities of certain tools (in this case, word-processing programs) to ensure rich response.

Although the story I have shared is situated in a specific context, most likely the challenges demonstrated by this story are not all that unusual, especially for first-time users of virtual peer review. In order to better accommodate the challenges of virtual peer review (and thus make virtual peer review less "abnormal"), we need more specific guidance. In the next chapter, I address more fully how to address these challenges by thinking in terms of our goals first and technology later—what I define as "technological flexibility." Given the concept of technological flexibility, I address strategies for conducting virtual peer review that take into account goals of the activity and technologies suited to those goals.

CHAPTER 5

Virtual Peer Review and Technological Flexibility

As the last chapter demonstrates, conducting virtual peer review with no guidance and without the help of distinctions regarding collaboration and technology can lead to challenges and frustrations. Moreover, because so many new online activities are introduced every year in relation to the Internet, it is critical to become more specific about what certain online activities entail. Such a level of detail is especially imperative in the case of virtual peer review, which, as I have argued throughout this book, may soon become a regular part of writing instruction in higher education. Writers using the Internet must become savvy, understanding the actions as well as responsibilities involved in certain Internet activities.

This chapter addresses the ways that virtual peer reviewers can become informed and educated about solid approaches to conducting virtual peer review—ways that allow writers to address challenges of collaboration and technology. Above all, addressing these challenges requires thinking critically about goals. As Burnett and Clark suggested, collaborative activities are often ill-defined; it is when we clearly articulate our goals for a collaborative activity that we are better able to integrate technologies. Throughout this chapter, then, I demonstrate virtual peer review according to scenarios in which various technologies may likely be used and easily integrated. In doing so, I suggest that virtual peer review can make use of several technologies (and take several forms) depending on the specific goals of a virtual peer review session. Therefore, the scenarios I describe are goal driven, in accordance with the idea that pedagogy must drive technology. In addition, each scenario includes actions, illustrating the argument that writing is *active and involved* rather than passive.

To some extent, the scenarios of virtual peer review I include here also address technological issues in computer pedagogy within writing studies. As I explained in chapter 1, the desire to explore technologies for writing instruction has generated enormous interest among scholars, some of whom have celebrated multiple and novel uses of technology for writing instruction. Here I do not advocate any one particular technology program or software; I deliberately avoid such advocacy in order to concentrate on pedagogical goals first and foremost. Rather, given the insight provided by Burnett and Clark about various factors involved in collaborative technologies, I approach the exploration of writing technologies in terms of what I call "technological flexibility," or the idea that writing activities should transcend any one particular technology. In the following section I explain this concept and its connections to virtual peer review and technological literacy.

Technological Flexibility

In chapter 4 I reviewed factors of collaboration suggested by Burnett and Clark that influence technology use and selection: group characteristics, group agreements, task characteristics, and technology environment. I applied these factors to virtual peer review to demonstrate that virtual peer review could be conducted in many ways. Here I suggest that such diversity of application—depending on a number of factors—can be defined more broadly in terms of "technological flexibility." Technological flexibility is a concept that addresses writing instruction or any other context in which a variety of technological tools exist to accomplish a writing task. By "technological flexibility," I mean that *the goals we have for writing tasks drive our choices and uses of technology.* In the context of writing instruction—the primary context with which I am concerned here—technological flexibility requires that an instructor consider the specific goals for instruction and identify the *range* of technologies that may be used to achieve those goals. The idea of technological flexibility therefore reflects the number of technological possibilities for instructional activities. As such, technological flexibility suggests that technology *respond* to goals and not the other way around; in theory and practice, technological flexibility affirms the guideline that pedagogy must drive technology. In addition, when technological flexibility exists, the expectation that activities must be tied to certain technologies dissolves.

The concept of technological flexibility can be a powerful tool for instructors designing computer-based writing activities. Rather than making choices based on the latest and greatest available software, instructors mindful of technological flexibility can consider all their options and make critical decisions about instructional technology. Keeping technological flexibility in mind can even simplify choices about instructional technology; as I suggested in chapter 4, virtual peer review can be conducted using simple e-mail and does not require any specially designed (or expensive) technology. And yet, in identifying a range of possible technologies, instructors have the option of trying more sophisticated options if they so desire and if means are available at their institution. Thinking about technological flexibility reminds us that technology exists in context, by which I mean that technology does not exist in a vacuum, but rather is wholly dependent on those who create it, use it, ignore it, or control it.

Technological flexibility in virtual peer review applies as well to students, for students must consider their technological options both inside and outside of the classroom. For example, students may be asked to complete virtual peer review outside of class. Thus, students must consider a number of factors: technologies that are available to them (both inside and outside the classroom); their level of familiarity with these technologies; the compatibility of technologies with peers; and goals for using technologies. In short, when students conduct virtual peer review, they must think carefully about the technology they are going to use for the activity. What I find so powerful about the concept of technological flexibility is the constant reminder that we can think critically about what we need, rather than let technologies determine our actions or lesson plans.

As a concept, then, technological flexibility implies *autonomy and critical thinking* with regard to technological choices. Consequently, technological flexibility goes hand in hand with technological literacy, or the ability to use technology and think about it critically (Selfe, *Technology and Literacy;* Gurak, *Cyberliteracy;* Dugger). Because I believe this connection between technological flexibility and technological literacy is crucially important, I'd like to spend more time addressing it here, but doing so first requires an understanding of "technological literacy," which is a complex term, to be sure. As Selfe explains in *Technology and Literacy in the Twenty-First Century,* the relationship between literacy and technology is extremely complicated:

> Technological literacy refers to a complex set of socially and culturally situated values, practices, and skills involved in operating linguistically within the context of electronic environments, including reading, writing, and communicating. The term further refers to the linking of technology and literacy at fundamental levels of both conception and social practice. (11)

In this definition, Selfe makes important distinctions: technological literacy does not refer only to the use of a computer, but also refers to the ability to think critically about technology, including its creation, contexts, and uses. As Selfe notes, this definition of technological literacy has extended our understanding of technological literacy beyond mere computer skills (10; see also Dugger). In *Cyberliteracy: Navigating the Internet with Awareness,* Gurak concurs, suggesting that definitions of technological literacy based on performance ("how to use a computer and keyboard") are inadequate (13). She suggests that we need "a new literacy, a critical literacy" in which we learn "not just how to use the technology but how to live with it, participate in it, and take control of it" (11). Several scholars have adopted this critical lens to explore various aspects of technology, such as technology creation (Haas); the influence of technology on workplace practices (Zuboff); instructional technology (Wahlstrom, "Teaching"; Mehlenbacher); and feminist and ideological perspectives of technology (Selfe, "Technology"; Warshauer; Wahlstrom, "Communication"). In addition, responsibilities of educators with regard to technological literacy have also been examined. Selfe argues, for example, that educators have a responsibility to promote technological literacy: "Literacy professionals and the organizations that represent them need to commit to understanding the complex relationship between literacy and technology and to intervening in the national project to expand technological literacy" (*Technology and Literacy* 160). To become technologically literate, according to these scholars, is to be aware of how technology both shapes and is shaped by social, political, economical, and cultural factors.

I suggest that the concept of technological flexibility is aligned with this definition of technological literacy, because it includes a range of technological options and it requires that users select technologies based on what would best fit their context and goals. Technological flexibility is a vehicle, if you will, for actualizing technological literacy. As I explain throughout this chapter, technological flexibility (and, consequently, technological literacy) are primary characteristics of virtual peer review, because the activity encourages students to think critically about context and what they want to accomplish in a virtual peer review session.

In exploring virtual peer review in terms of technological flexibility, then, it is necessary first to identify the range of technological options available to students and instructors. In chapter 4 I reviewed possibilities in terms of synchronous and asynchronous technologies, but here I situate those technologies in terms of general categories described by Bonk and King in *Electronic Collaborators*. Bonk and King describe three categories of technologies that I find useful in relation to virtual peer review: stand-alone system collaboration, asynchronous electronic processing, and multiconferencing (xxviii–xxxii). Stand-alone system collaboration, they say, is the "most common but least elegant form of computer-supported collaboration: pairs of teams of students working together at a single workstation or sharing a common computer" (xxviii). Asynchronous electronic processing is "asynchronous conferencing and electronic mail systems (E-mail)" (xxix). Multiconferencing is "synchronous or real-time conferencing" (xxxii).

These general categories can all relate to virtual peer review, although stand-alone collaboration is perhaps the least common because it involves more face-to-face communication than online communication. (However, stand-alone collaboration may be useful when first introducing students to virtual peer review.) Categories of asynchronous conferencing and synchronous conferencing are the most likely technologies for virtual peer review, and they vary in the degree to which interaction is delayed among virtual peer reviewers. For example, using asynchronous conferencing such as e-mail or programs that facilitate e-mail exchange (like bulletin boards or group pages in WebCT or Blackboard), virtual peer reviewers will notice a pronounced delay in interaction, sometimes spanning days. Using synchronous conferencing such as chats, MOOs, MUDs, IRC, or Instant Messaging (IM), virtual peer reviewers will notice communication that more closely resembles a live discussion, although even synchronous conferencing experiences delays ranging from two seconds to up to a minute (Dillenbourg 8).

As I describe the various scenarios for virtual peer review, I will reference one of these general technological categories. Because the purpose of my discussion here is not to review technologies, I refrain from evaluating any specific program within these general categories. Given this explanation of technological flexibility and the range of possible technologies for virtual peer review, in the remainder of this chapter I share scenarios of virtual peer review in an effort to more fully illustrate how virtual peer review can be conducted as an instructional activity. Each scenario describes a specific pedagogical goal related to virtual peer review, actions required to fulfill that goal, technological recommendations, and suggestions for preparing students. The scenarios are meant to provide specific guidance for what students can do in virtual peer review and the technologies that can be easily integrated. In describing these scenarios, I am also mindful of the differences of time, space, and interaction that I addressed in chapter 2; because of these differences, I do not claim that the scenarios of virtual peer review are in any way better than face-to-face peer review. On the contrary, my aim is to contribute to our understanding of how virtual interactions may be used for peer review. Because the scenarios I describe are goal driven, virtual peer review may look different from one session to the next depending on the goals selected for the given session and the technologies that best facilitate those goals. The idea is to encourage virtual peer reviewers to always think of their goals first and then select technologies that are best suited to those goals.[1]

Scenario One: Substantive Intertextual Comments

Imagine you wanted feedback on a specific aspect of your writing, perhaps to trace a thesis statement and its support throughout a paper you have written. It would be particularly helpful if you could receive feedback that directly addresses passages in your text that relate to your thesis. In this type of scenario, where direct feedback on specific passages is desired, virtual peer review could be conducted using "substantive intertextual comments." Substantive intertextual comments are comments made by reviewers that are placed right next to passages of the text in question. The term "intertextual" is one I borrow from Barbara Monroe, who suggests that intertextual comments are useful for blunt response to passages (she uses the term "red-line" [15]). While Monroe suggests that intertextual comments are most useful for corrections, they can also play a much broader role, such as providing reader response and reactions not just to errors, but to content and organization, purpose, style, and other factors as specified by the author. The *goal* of substantive intertextual comments, then, is to provide detailed reader response to specific passages in an author's writing. When intertextual commentary is provided by more than one reviewer, authors are exposed to individual interpretations of their writing and suggestions for improvement. Intertextual comments thus provide a powerful form of response that gives authors an idea of how their writing has been understood by readers and how specific passages may be improved.

The *actions* involved in intertextual comments are reading, writing, and interacting. That is, while reading an author's writing, students must simultaneously decide what comments to write in the text. In doing so, they interact on two levels: (1) the reviewer literally interacts with the author's text by placing comments next to passages of interest; (2) the reviewer interacts with the author as he or she writes comments with the author in mind. Thus, substantive intertextual comments reflect what Bolter has identified as "intertextuality" or connections between readers, authors, and texts (163). In fact, to some degree, in virtual peer review an author's writing becomes destabilized as virtual peer reviewers comment online. As Bolter suggests, "Electronic text is the first text in which the elements of meaning, of structure, and of visual display are fundamentally unstable" (31). In writing intertextual comments, peer reviewers add to a text, creating a new document that includes their response. Student roles thus become more fluid; they become both reviewers and writers in the activity of virtual peer review, shifting in and out of reading, writing, and interactive response.[2]

However, those students new to virtual peer review may resist this new way of responding because of their unfamiliarity with reading and writing simultaneously online. For example, in a study of online tutors, Sam Racine and I discovered that tutors resisted responding directly online. It happened that tutors printed student papers, wrote responses by hand, and then returned to the computer to *retype* their comments in electronic form so they could send them to students. Such a finding told us two things: (1) tutors were not yet comfortable reading and responding online and defaulted to handwritten response; (2) responding both in handwriting and online doubled and sometimes tripled response time (Breuch and Racine). Responding in handwriting *and* online appears to be an extremely inefficient practice; instructors who assign online intertextual comments would benefit from encouraging students to read and write directly online.

Because intertextual comments require a close reading of an author's writing, as well as placement of comments directly in a text, technologies best suited for this type of response include word processing and asynchronous technologies. A typical procedure for intertextual comments might involve a reviewer entering comments to an author's document, saving the document as a new document that includes peer comments, and sending that document back to the author as an attachment to an e-mail message.[3] Within word-processing programs, students can enter intertextual comments in a variety of ways: through footnotes, "tools," or interruptions of the text using a symbol or different font or style to indicate their comments (like asterisks **). Or, using e-mail, an author may include key passages in the text of an e-mail message, and reviewers can make intertextual comments directly in the e-mail text. See figure 20 for examples of these types of intertextual comments. Although intertextual comments are characterized by their direct placement next to passages in question, some find the practice intrusive. To accommodate an author or reviewer who resists such blatant interruptions in a text, some programs allow reviewers to note responses in less intrusive ways, such as through pop-up windows or the use of symbols. See figure 21 for examples. Specially designed programs that accommodate peer review (such as WebConnect) also take this approach, by inserting symbols that signal a comment from a reviewer.

Asynchronous technologies provide clear advantages for intertextual commentary. As Walther notes, one advantage of using asynchronous technologies is that students have more time to read and reflect. Rather than read and respond on the spot, reviewers have time to carefully consider their responses to certain passages. Another advantage of asynchronous technologies for intertextual commentary is that responses from peer reviewers need not be limited by page space; reviewers can write responses as long or as short as they like. This flexibility is perhaps one of the great advantages of commenting online. As Bolter remarks, "[A] text in electronic space has no necessary margins, no fixed boundaries except for the ultimate limitations of the machine" (163). In virtual environments, peers can shape their comments in many ways to maximize response.

To illustrate intertextual comments, consider the example in figure 22. To enhance the use of intertextual comments, reviewers should be encouraged to read and write onscreen rather than print. In addition, reviewers may find a timeline for completion useful in the case that asynchronous response requires more time to complete.

Scenario Two: Chat Responses to Author Queries

Imagine you are in a peer response group and you've already received feedback from your reviewers, but you'd like to continue the discussion because you

Footnotes

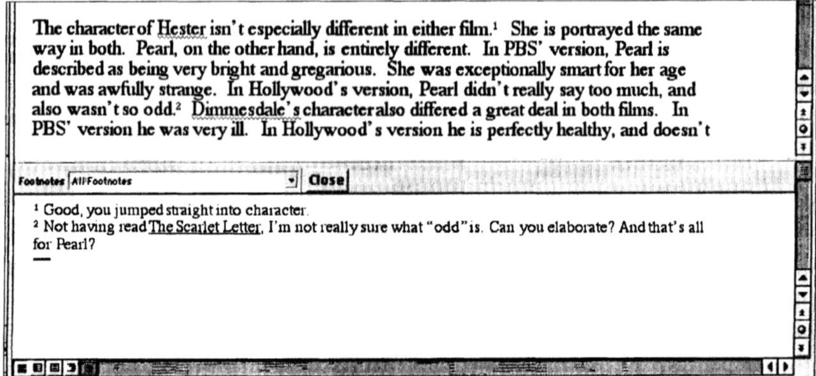

"Tools"

today. The group in many ways resembles some of the traits of More's Utopia as well as
the Oneida community. ~~The Lost Valley's communal aspects can clearly relate to both
groups.~~ Unity is very important in the ~~community~~Lost Valley. Everyday is begun with a
meeting and the joining

Asterisks

There are a few likenesses and many differences from group to group, but they share

in some common basic traditions, blue-printed by More's Utopia, including a sense of

dissatisfaction from the outside society, a common view, **a common view of . . .

what?** and some version of a communal aspect of life.

Figure 20. Options for Substantive Intertextual Comments

have more questions for reviewers. One of those questions pertains to your
overall approach to documentation. You'd like to know: Have you used the
assigned format correctly? Was your approach to parenthetical citations correct? You also have some other questions you'd like to ask your reviewers about
their responses. You post your questions to your group on e-mail, but because
reviewers enter the e-mail conversation at different times, and because group
members are busy with their own paper revisions, your post remains unan-
swered (in fact, because reviewers have already provided feedback, they may

Symbols

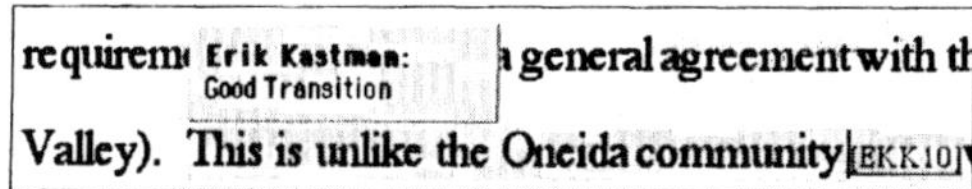

Pop-up Windows

Figure 21. Nonintrusive Methods for Substantive Intertextual Comments

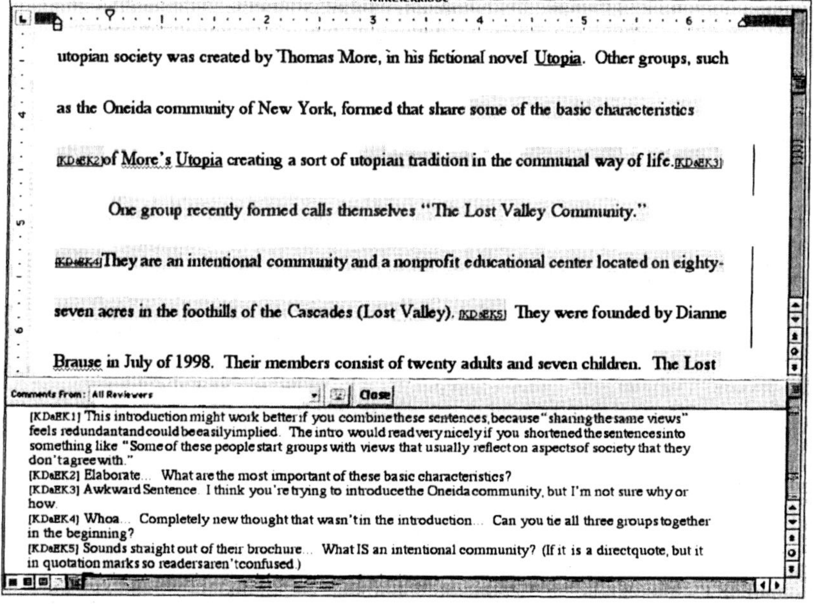

Figure 22. Sample Use of Substantive Intertextual Comments

think their work is done). In a study of online peer review, Beth Hewett encountered exactly this scenario: after initial reviews, additional author queries were frequently ignored; she also found that asynchronous technologies contributed to the problem. Students in her study expressed frustration about this aspect of virtual peer review, for students expected that reviewers would be accessible beyond the initial virtual peer review to continue the discussion.

In the case that authors have queries for members of their group, virtual peer review may be conducted through chat responses. The *goal* of such sessions would be to continue peer review discussion by providing quick, direct responses to author queries. Another goal of this scenario is to provide multiple responses to author queries. In this way, chat responses can create a supportive environment for authors; a safe place to share concerns about their writing and receive response and suggestions from other group members.

The *actions* involved in chat responses include conversing online and following a question-and-answer format. It is useful if chats are highly structured—that is, organized around an author's queries—and that all members understand that the purpose of the chat is to respond to questions. It is also useful if, in chat responses, the author facilitates the online discussion, leading with his or her questions. That is to say, during chat responses to author queries the author "has the floor," so to speak. Chats can be arranged around a single author, or they can be arranged so that each group member gets an allotted time during the chat to post his or her queries and receive direct feedback from the rest of the group (each member gets a chance to "have the floor"). Granting authors the role of discussion facilitator is an important factor of this type of virtual peer review, for it encourages the author to take an active role in asking their questions and receiving feedback. In this way, author queries exemplify active learning in online environments, because authors take responsibility for shaping virtual peer review sessions and asking for feedback.

Clearly, the best technology for chat responses to author queries is synchronous chats that allow for discussion among several group members. Asynchronous technologies may be used, too, for author queries, but may be easier to ignore. When members of peer review groups receive author queries by e-mail, as Beth Hewett found, group members may be selective about their responses, and simply ignore what they do not care to (or know how to) address. The advantage of synchronous technology in this scenario is that members are more likely to respond to author queries in a real-time discussion than to ignore them. In this way, synchronous chats may hold the attention of group members and focus their attention more fully on the author's query.

There are a variety of ways such chats can be arranged: through IRC, MUDs, or any chat room offered by Internet providers (AOL, Yahoo, etc.).

Chats can also be set up using integrated Web courseware programs such as WebCT and Blackboard.com. Using these programs, students must have access to their course space, and can simply go to the chat function and select a room to "meet." (See figure 23.)

Scenario Three: Summary Endnotes with Suggestions for Change

Imagine that you wanted an overall sense of your reviewers' impression of your writing, including a summary of any major changes that the reviewers have suggested. You hope to receive reviews that note strong as well as weak points,

Samantha: Thanks for meeting, everybody. Can you all help me?

Scott: What is your question?

Samantha: I am having trouble with documentation.

Lisa: We're using MLA, right?

Josh: Yep.

Lisa: OK, Sam, what is your question?

Samantha: When you use a citation in the paper, what information needs to go into the parentheses?

Scott: Author and date

Josh: Author and page number

Lisa: Just a minute I have it right here

Samantha: I had author and year, but I think that is wrong.

Lisa: The handbook says it depends on if the author is mentioned in the text already. If it is, then you only need to cite the page number in the parentheses.

Scott: What about the year?

Lisa: I think that the author's name is the main reference that is needed, and then page number for exact quote.

Josh: That sounds right to me

Samantha: OK, thanks, everyone!

Figure 23. Sample "Author Query" Chat

and you also hope to receive specific suggestions for change. In addition, you want to quickly grasp reviewers' suggestions, rather than read through detailed intertextual comments throughout. Virtual peer review in this case can be conducted by providing what Barbara Monroe has called an "end note," or a comment found at the end of a document that summarizes a reviewer's response and suggestions for revision (22). As I mentioned in chapter 4, endnotes were the most common form of virtual peer review comments in the class I observed. This form of response should be familiar to many (both students and teachers alike), for it is also commonly employed by instructors in the evaluation of student papers. In fact, much research has been conducted on this form of instructor response to student writing, specifically to explore the usefulness of such comments in helping students strengthen their writing. Incidentally, some scholars have suggested that endnote comments are most helpful when they support what was done well and when they offer concrete suggestions for improvement. However, while instructor endnote responses have been a frequent topic of research, few if any studies explore the usefulness of *student* endnote responses in helping other students improve writing. To this end, it is important to note that some scholars have doubted the usefulness of student comments at all (Peckham; Bruffee, "Conversation"; Newkirk), for students may have difficulty identifying weaknesses in other students' papers, or may not know what or how to provide specific directions for revision. Such issues have not been explored to the same degree with regard to virtual peer review; only a handful of researchers have begun to address how student summary responses may be useful in virtual environments. For example, in a qualitative study of four student writers using online peer review, Mabrito found that students tended to provide more directive criticism in virtual environments than in face-to-face environments.

The *goal* of summary endnotes, then, is to provide an overall summary of strengths and weaknesses, and to provide suggestions for improvement. In essence, endnotes are a place to articulate criticism in a constructive way. Thus, while endnotes may be a common form of virtual peer review, they are difficult to articulate, especially when students may feel they do not want to hurt the feelings of other students. As Bruffee suggests, "[W]ritten peer criticism is the most difficult writing any student will ever do because it is the most *real* writing most students ever do as students" (emphasis his, *Short Course* 115). In this statement, Bruffee suggests that audience is clearly a factor in writing peer criticism, because students are given the task of providing honest and constructive feedback directly to the author. To avoid any harsh feelings, students may provide general or vague comments in endnotes such as "sounds good." But strong endnotes require that students go beyond general or vague comments. Instead, students must learn to support their comments with detail, even in the cases when they compliment the author.

The *actions* required for endnotes basically involve writing one or several paragraphs at the end of an electronic document. To make the most out of endnotes, however, it is useful if student reviewers have already read through the author's paper, and perhaps made some intertextual comments throughout. Doing so would keep track of any suggestions or comments so that it is easier to recall them for a summary in an endnote. In addition, reviewing intertextual comments in preparation for an endnote may help reviewers track any patterns in the author's writing related to word-level, organization, or content issues. Again, it is important that students offer specific examples, whether in reference to positive or constructive comments. Keeping these suggestions in mind, students may write endnotes addressing the following prompts:

"What has the author done well?"
"What needs to be improved?"
"What suggestions can you offer to help the author?"

To provide even more specific feedback, endnotes can be tailored to the criteria specified by the instructor for a particular assignment.

Because endnotes require that reviewers reflect on their overall impression of an author's writing, asynchronous technologies are most useful, because they allow more time for reviewers to reflect and to articulate their suggestions. Reviewers may generate an endnote in the form of an e-mail message, or reviewers may enter an endnote directly at the end of a student's word document. Some scholars recommend asynchronous technologies for endnote comments because they may be more directive (Mabrito, "Electronic Mail"; Hewett); asynchronous technologies also allow reviewers to articulate endnotes in full without the interruption of other voices, as would occur in synchronous chats. In addition, reviewers may feel more comfortable providing endnotes asynchronously as opposed to synchronously. Sirc and Reynolds discovered, for example, that peer reviewers had a more difficult time sharing directive comments for revision in synchronous chats, for they were concerned about "saving face" in front of other group members online. While this reaction may be more characteristic of novice than experienced writers, it is something to consider in a student environment. Asynchronously, reviewers can reflect about their overall impressions and may feel more free to give their honest suggestions for revision. (See figure 24.)

Scenario Four: Brainstorming Ways to Improve Writing

Imagine that you prefer peer review sessions that occur in person because you like receiving collective feedback all in one time period; however, you are in a

Megan,
      You have set up a good compare-contrast paper that is chock full of wonderful examples of differences between the two versions of <u>The Scarlet</u> Letter. However, I find myself wishing you would use those examples sometimes. You have enough about character here to write a book. I think you should choose one or two characters, tell their differences, and then get into WHY PBS and Hollywood portray these people in such different lights. Is it more profitable to have a healthy Dimmesdale, because the audience can look up to him? Was it worthwhile creating a larger role for the actress who played Mistress Hibbons in order to sacrifice the integrity of the work? How do the changed characters contribute to the changed theme that you discuss at the end of the paper? Anyway, you have a well-crafted paper, with a whole lot of potential. Good luck.
-Erik

Figure 24. Sample Summary Endnote with Suggestions for Change

situation in which peer review is expected, but no meeting time has been provided for the activity. You also have a short time period to conduct peer review and to incorporate suggestions in a revision; furthermore, you are reluctant to use e-mail for peer review, because you are not sure you will hear from your peer reviewers in time to complete your revisions. In this scenario, virtual peer review sessions may be best conducted through a brainstorming chat using synchronous technologies.

A brainstorming chat is an exercise in which all authors receive feedback from other reviewers about their writing; it is perhaps the closest thing to a face-to-face peer review session in that all members meet together to discuss one another's writing. Indeed, synchronous technologies provide the closest semblance to live discussions. Brainstorming chats are also similar to author queries (scenario two), in that they may act as a type of support group for authors. But unlike author query chats, which are highly structured and facilitated by the author, brainstorming chats open the floor to all reviewers. That is, in brainstorming chats, all reviewers are encouraged to share their feedback on an author's writing, and the author may sit back to observe their comments. Thus, brainstorming chats tend to be less structured than author queries. Discussion may be organized according to author (fifteen minutes for each student, for example), but reviewers may chime in at any given moment. Indeed, reviewers may piggyback on the comments of other reviewers, and perhaps brainstorm suggestions for ways the author can address a particular issue. The result is an active discussion led by reviewers for the benefit of the author.

The *goal* of a brainstorming chat, then, is to provide collective, interactive feedback and to do so in a specified time period. Thus, the primary *actions* required to conduct brainstorming chats are interaction and discussion. When group members meet for the chat, they should be ready to jump into the discussion and offer comments and suggestions for each author. Because interaction and discussion are the primary actions required for this scenario, a brainstorming chat may *appear* to be the most intuitive form of virtual peer review; after all, it seeks to mimic the kinds of discussion that would occur in a face-to-face peer review session. However, I argue that brainstorming chats are the most difficult and challenging form of virtual peer review, because they are the least structured. I recall a time when I asked students to conduct brainstorming chats in their peer review groups, only to find that group members found chats an opportunity to outdo each other in telling jokes and creating pictures using the drawing tools provided in a white board for the chat. While students got very little accomplished in those chats, they created unmistakable bonds among their group members (in fact, they often described such chats as "fun"). Sirc and Reynolds discovered that novice writers often used chats in similar ways, suggesting that chats were great for building community. While such bonding may be great for student peer review groups, we must ask whether or not this result will help students accomplish the goal of the scenario I have described: to provide collective, interactive feedback about a student's writing.

If peer review groups hope to accomplish these goals using brainstorming chats, they may find it useful to impose some kind of structure on the chat—again, selecting a chat facilitator who keeps the discussion on track and notifies participants about time limits for discussing each student's writing. In addition, reviewers must come to the session prepared, having read the writing of all authors who will be reviewed in the session. It is also helpful if groups plan chats in advance so that all members are aware of the time and technology to be used for the chat (if they are to be conducted outside of class). Without such measures, brainstorming chats can easily give way to off-task chatter and result in a peer review session that may be a lot of fun, but may not help authors in receiving useful feedback about their writing. (See figure 25.)

Scenario Five: Evaluation

Imagine that you have been instructed not only to respond to another author's writing, but also to evaluate it. Although you are not sure that you have the perspective to evaluate another author's writing, the instructor or supervisor has provided an online form for you that addresses certain criteria. With the prompts provided, you feel more comfortable at least in knowing what to look for in another author's paper, but you also feel more anxiety about how your writing will be rated. In addition, you have been informed that your performance as a peer reviewer will be evaluated.

Unlike previous scenarios of virtual peer review that give authors and reviewers great latitude with regard to the content of their comments, this scenario of virtual peer review purposefully directs student comments. Thus, the

Tyler: So, has anyone begun their paper yet?
Carol: I have a draft of mine . . . aren't we supposed to?
Tom: I have a few ideas.
Tyler: What are we supposed to talk about in here?
Tom: I don't know, maybe something about our paper ideas.
Carol: I think we are supposed to help with paper topics.
Carol: So, what are your paper topics?
Tom: Mine is about the logging industry
Tyler: I don't have one yet. Any ideas? Ha ha
Carol: Logging industry . . . what about?
Tom: Whether or not it is good to harvest trees that have been burned in forest fires.
Carol: Oh that's right, you're a Forestry major, aren't you?
Tyler: Hey, I have an idea for my paper. How about debate about the use of sport enhancing drugs?
Tom: That sounds like a good idea Tyler, what would you do with it?
Tyler: I don't know, maybe discuss the pros and cons
Carol: You could pull in some examples from the news about athletes who have failed drug tests
Tom: Maybe look at Olympic athletes
Tyler: Oh, that's a good idea, thanks!

Figure 25. Sample Brainstorming Chat

goal of evaluative virtual peer review is to direct response to specific evaluative criteria. There are both advantages and disadvantages to this approach. One advantage is that exposing students to criteria helps them develop a vocabulary they can use as they discuss writing; when asked to apply that criteria to other students' work, they reinforce that criteria for their own writing. In addition, students become more familiar with the standards instructors have for evaluation of writing. Including evaluation as part of virtual peer review also suggests a level of accountability that may not exist in other forms of peer review; that is, when students know their peer reviews will be examined by an instructor, they may take more care in writing comments. A disadvantage of virtual peer review as evaluation, however, is that requiring students to evaluate other students may cause great anxiety and may actually stifle the quality of response in virtual peer review. Students may argue that they are not in a position to evaluate other student work, and they may suggest that doing so places them in a very uncomfortable position. Consequently, they may be more lenient in their ratings of other students than they would be if they were free to offer directive criticism in other forms. In addition, some scholars have suggested that having students evaluate each other misses the point of providing thorough reader response, which is not always dictated by clear criteria. Ultimately, instructors must make the choice whether or not to include evaluation as an aspect of virtual peer review.

The *action* involved in evaluative peer review is decision-making. It is not enough to respond to the author; in this scenario, reviewers must also make judgments about how well the author has fulfilled specified criteria. Given that reviewers must take time to make decisions about other students' writing, synchronous technologies would not be appropriate for evaluative virtual peer review. However, a wide range of other technologies could be employed, ranging from word processing to specially designed software programs. Instructors might create an online worksheet (similar to print worksheets that may be used in face-to-face peer review) that guides the response of students in their peer reviews. If made available electronically, such as through shared file space, reviewers could complete the forms online and submit them electronically both to the instructor and the author. Evaluative peer review could also be facilitated through e-mail or Web-based surveys, in which reviewers rate an author's work by clicking on ratings specified in an online form. (See figure 26.) Specially designed programs for evaluative peer review may integrate these approaches, such as the program Calibrated Peer Review (CPR™), in which students are guided through a "training module" for peer review. When first entering this program, students are asked to read a paper that the instructor has posted and rate that paper according to specified criteria (the Web program enables a split screen, in which one screen shows the paper and the other shows the online rating form). Students also can enter comments as they conduct their rating. When finished with this tutorial, they are shown their ratings next to the instructor's rating of the same paper, thus showing how well a student's rating "calibrates" with an instructor's rating. The design is quite clever in that students can have a clearer idea of instructor expectations for their own writing. The program also maintains the activity of virtual peer review quite well, keeping students accountable for the activity and giving instructors detailed information about student reactions to other student writing. In addition, instructors can quantify virtual peer review through the ratings students provide; as such, the program has been very popular in empirical sciences

Peer Review Evaluation Criteria for Assignment #4

Reviewer: **Author:**

Category	Explanation	Check: Has the author addressed these aspects in their paper?
Content	Address topic, purpose, rationale, and audience of assignment #6; include outline of proposed paper as well as bibliographical sources.	
Purpose	Preview your plan for assignment #6 in a succinct form.	
Audience	Write for instructor and teaching assistants in Rhet 1101.	
Organization	Use sections and headings for topic, purpose, rationale, and audience. Include outline for content of assignment #6.	
Design	Use the following format: typed and double-spaced text, with no more than 1-inch margins on all sides.	
Support	Include list of sources, in bibliographical MLA form, that you plan to use for assignment #6.	
Expression	Use complete sentences, correct mechanics, and correct grammar.	

Comments:

Figure 26. Sample Evaluation Sheet for Virtual Peer Review

Table 4
Virtual Peer Review Goal-Driven Scenarios

Scenario	Goal	Action(s)	Technology	Rationale
Substantive Intertextual Comments	To provide detailed reader response to specific passages	Reading, writing, and interacting online	Asynchronous (e-mail; word-processing tools; software for inserting comments or footnotes)	Asynchronous technologies allow reviewers more time for detailed reflection and commentary
Chat Responses to Author Queries	To continue peer review discussion by providing quick, direct responses to specific author queries	Conversing online, following a question-and-answer format	Synchronous (chat rooms in Web courseware programs; MOO or MUD chats, IRC)	Synchronous technologies encourage reviewers to provide quick, direct responses when prompted by the author
Summary Endnotes	To provide an overall summary of strengths and weaknesses, and suggestions for improvement	Writing, reflecting, summarizing	Asynchronous (e-mail; word-processing tools; software for inserting comments or footnotes)	Asynchronous technologies allow reviewers to articulate constructive criticism more fully than synchronous technologies do
Brainstorming Chats	To provide collective, interactive feedback and suggestions to an author	Interacting, discussing	Synchronous (chat rooms in Web courseware programs; MOO or MUD chats, IRC)	Synchronous technologies allow multiple voices to interact, perhaps building on one another's suggestions
Evaluating Writing	To direct response to specific evaluative criteria	Decision-making, reflection, critical thinking	Asynchronous (e-mail; word-processing tools; software for online evaluation [CPR])	Asynchronous technologies allow reviewers more time to make evaluative decisions on peers' writing

that have writing-intensive requirements (fields such as chemistry, physics, and biology). The program provides tangible feedback and also concrete measurements for peer review, and does so in a way that is convenient and manageable in a virtual environment.

Applying Scenarios and Technological Flexibility

What I hope this chapter demonstrates is that conducting virtual peer review requires thoughtful planning and careful reading and responding on the part of the reviewer. In addition, because computers are a factor in virtual peer review, reviewers must be purposeful and strategic in their uses of technology. They must think critically and take control of technology. They also must make choices, not only about the technology they use, but also about their goals for using technology in the first place. Thus, in the context of a classroom, virtual peer review exemplifies the kind of technological literacy espoused by Selfe, Gurak, and others: not only the ability to use technology, but to take control of it and to think critically about it. In addition, such flexibility demonstrates that virtual peer review sessions may not look the same from one to the next—they do not rely on one form of communication, such as face-to-face talking—but rather rely on a host of activities including reading, writing, interacting, discussing, and decision-making. And of course, these different kinds of feedback can all be electronically recorded for future reference. Table 4 illustrates how virtual peer review illustrates technological flexibility and critical thinking about technology. Seen in this way, virtual peer review illustrates how a pedagogical activity can drive technology and not the other way around.

Implications of Virtual Peer Review for the Writing Classroom and Beyond

Throughout this book I have argued that virtual peer review is a remediation of peer review, and I have outlined the ways in which computer technology has the potential to change and shape peer review response. In essence, virtual peer review emphasizes written communication over oral communication, and it illuminates writing as an act of involvement through reading, writing, and interacting online. These aspects of virtual peer review fundamentally differ from peer review as it has been documented in writing studies; that is, as primarily an exercise of oral communication.

Because computer technology introduces changes in the activity of peer review, virtual peer review is also a remediation of peer review in the sense that it has overarching implications for writing studies. As I have suggested here, much peer review literature has focused on the connections between peer review and social theories of language—social construction in particular (Bruffee, "Conversation"; Gere; Spigelman; DiPardo and Freedman; Spear, *Sharing Writing*). Early discussions of virtual peer review draw on these connections, suggesting that virtual peer review can be justified by the ways in which computer technology (online chats and interaction) reinforces social theories of language (Barker and Kemp; Skubikowski and Elder; Cyganowski; Palmquist). However, I argue that virtual peer review offers much more to our understanding of peer review in writing studies. In addition to reinforcing social theories of language, virtual peer review contributes to our understanding of technological literacy, which is a crucial issue in writing studies today, particularly as computers become more a part of our writing practices. Thus, in support of scholars who have asserted that technological literacy is a responsibility among writing scholars and teachers (Selfe, *Technology and Literacy*; Tornow; Gurak, *Cyberliteracy*; Haas), I argue that virtual peer review is one way we may begin to integrate technological literacy into writing studies. Specifically, virtual peer review can be integrated as a computer-based writing activity into the following contexts: writing pedagogy; online writing centers; writing-across-the-curriculum; and workplace settings. In this chapter, I discuss ways that virtual peer review may contribute to the drive to integrate technology into writing practices.

Writing Pedagogy

In chapter 1 I suggested that computer-based instruction has been an area of writing studies that is fraught with complex issues and attitudes. Here I fully endorse the perspective that writing instructors have a *responsibility* to integrate computer technology into their writing courses. While I acknowledge the challenges that accompany this responsibility, I suggest that virtual peer review can play a transitional role: it can help instructors transition to computer-based classrooms, especially since it has grounding in peer review and pedagogical assumptions important to writing pedagogy. In this section, then, I observe two ways that instructors can integrate technology into writing classrooms: (1) by assigning virtual peer review, and (2) by evaluating student writing using virtual peer review methods.

Assigning Virtual Peer Review

Assigning virtual peer review is one way that instructors can accentuate writing classes with technology. Here I propose an assignment model in which virtual peer review becomes a recurring activity in the writing classroom (see figure 27). One advantage of conducting virtual peer review on a recurring basis is that it fosters a consistent use of technology for the purpose of improving writing. This application is important, considering the vast array of options instructors have for implementing computers in writing classrooms. As I suggested in chapter 1, as the field of computers and writing grows, so grows the number of computer applications as well as theoretical complexities about using computers. Although there are several interesting assignments that make use of various computer technologies, virtual peer review offers an alternative to isolated computer-based activities. That is, virtual peer review offers a thorough approach to integrating computers in the classroom, because it can be assigned consistently—much like face-to-face peer review—for every writing assignment. Assigning virtual peer review on a recurring basis also allows students the opportunity to practice using technology and to find methods of peer response that work well for them.

As figure 27 describes, if virtual peer review is to be practiced regularly by students, it should be introduced early in a course. Instructors can prepare for virtual peer review by assigning long-term student groups and creating some kind of electronic space for virtual peer review (such as networked computers, group spaces in programs such as Blackboard.com or WebCT, or a course listserv). When practiced consistently throughout a course, instructors should spend at least one class period introducing students to virtual peer review and allowing them to practice the activity in the classroom (employing what Bonk and King refer to as a "stand-alone system" of collaboration).

Instructors can also specify, after this point, whether virtual peer review will be practiced regularly inside or outside of class.

Although I have defined virtual peer review as an exclusively online activity, instructors should be encouraged to explore variations of the activity to suit their specific instructional contexts. For example, virtual peer review can be a supplement to face-to-face peer review sessions, it can be integrated into a face-to-face computer lab environment, or it can be conducted outside of class entirely. Or instructors can implement a combination of all three. The model I describe is one that can be easily adapted to computer-lab virtual peer reviews or out-of-class virtual peer reviews. This model emphasizes, above all, that instructors should carefully plan for virtual peer review rather than attempt it as a last-minute exercise (note that the first four steps of the model I propose involve planning). Again, as figure 27 indicates, it is especially important to devote *at least one class day* to preparing students for the activity, reviewing goals for the workshop and introducing students to the technologies that will be used.

In addition, it is imperative that instructors familiarize students with two key aspects of peer review before plunging into the activity: (1) reviewer and author roles and (2) constructive criticism. Because these aspects are already important in face-to-face and virtual peer review, instructors and students may already be familiar with these aspects. However, these aspects change slightly when practiced in the virtual medium, so it is important to review these changes. I address them briefly here.

In any kind of peer review, the *author role* involves bringing writing to the group members and specifying areas he or she believes need improvement in the paper. The *reviewer role,* then, involves reading an author's writing and providing comments about areas specified by the author, as well as general reader response to the author's writing. The general intent of these roles remains true for both face-to-face and virtual forms of peer review, although they are practiced differently. In face-to-face environments, workshops could be configured so that the reviewer and author simply discuss the author's writing (reading must be done before the actual discussion). But face-to-face workshops could also require the author to read aloud his or her writing to peer groups and to receive direct response as they are reading.

In virtual peer review, the author role involves providing one's writing to the peer group, but the author must do so electronically, either by posting the word-processed document in a networked classroom (as Barker and Kemp describe), sending an e-mail message to peers with an attachment, or using Web-based integrated software that allows for group space and document exchange (through programs like WebCT and Blackboard). As authors post their writing, it is important that they also articulate, in writing, areas that they would like reviewers to address. They may place this explanatory

1. Assign student groups for the semester/quarter (groups would not change). Having students work in the same groups will allow students the chance to better develop a supportive writing community, through both face-to-face and online interactions. (Inae Kang's findings suggest that online groups form better interpersonal relationships when they are long-term—1998.)

2. Create a space for students to conduct virtual peer review. Options include establishing an e-mail listserv for an entire class or for separate groups; creating group space through "Group Pages" in Blackboard.com or a similar function in WebCT; using network file-sharing among classroom computers (usually this service is handled by university computer administrators). If none of these options is available, students can conduct virtual peer review through simple e-mail and attachments, although instructors must first investigate whether or not all students have access to e-mail and computer technology outside of class.

3. Introduce students to the idea of peer review and evaluation criteria. Scholarship about connections between peer review and social theories of learning provide a helpful background to the activity. In addition, instructors should introduce students to important aspects of peer review, including reviewer and author roles and constructive feedback.

4. Consider specific goals for your virtual peer review workshop (i.e., providing detailed intertextual commentary; providing summary comments; discussing online; evaluating other students' writing) and select a technology appropriate to that goal (synchronous chats, asynchronous messages, word processing, or other programs). For an overview of technological options, see chapter 4 of this book. If possible, include models of virtual peer review workshops; options may include sharing a print account of one of your own virtual peer review workshops or having students bring in examples of times they have received constructive feedback online about their writing.

5. Conduct the first peer review in class in a computer lab using word-processing or other selected software to introduce students to computer technology in an environment where they can receive help from instructors and peers. This step will also allow students to meet and work with their group members face-to-face and get accustomed to the technology.

6. Conduct the second peer review outside of class, having students use asynchronous or synchronous technologies to exchange writing and send feedback to one another.

    Asynchronous—Students would write drafts using word-processing software; students would attach a document to an e-mail message, with a message to reviewer(s) to review the paper and identifying at least two areas about

Figure 27. Suggestions for Implementing Virtual Peer Review
(continued on next page)

which they would like feedback. Reviewers would receive the document when they check their e-mail; read the message from the author; read the document; comment using BOLD or some other font style; reviewers would send the document back to the author as an e-mail attachment, along with a message explaining overall comments and suggestions. (This option requires that students have access to word processing and e-mail. Instructors may wish to set up separate listservs for each review group.)

Synchronous—A student pair or group would exchange documents and read them previous to the synchronous discussion; students would plan a time to meet in an online chat; students would have a discussion about the documents, following standard author/reviewer roles. (This option requires that students have access to one of these technologies: (1) a chat room associated with the writing class; (2) a MOO or MUD where they can meet online.)

7. Assign virtual peer reviews for consecutive assignments. If desired, virtual peer reviews can be collected and handed in by students for purposes of instructor records or evaluation of virtual peer review.

Figure 27 *(continued)*

comment at the beginning of their document or type it in an e-mail message to which their document is attached. The reviewer role in virtual peer review, then, requires that the reviewer access the electronic document (through word-processing or e-mail text), read it online, and decide upon a method of commentary—either synchronous or asynchronous commentary. If the reviewer chooses asynchronous methods, they can write their comments directly in the author's text. As I explained in chapters 2 and 5, there are several methods for inserting electronic comments, and reviewers can decide which method they prefer. However, this reviewer role means that the reviewer bears all responsibility for all commentary (it does not occur within a discussion). Synchronous forms of virtual peer review require that the reviewer read the electronic document submitted by the author and be prepared to discuss the writing in an interactive online discussion.

Constructive criticism is another important aspect of peer review conducted virtually. As some scholars have noted, peer review response may not be all that helpful when peers do not offer criticism or when they do not know what feedback to offer. In fact, it is quite common to hear what I call the "sounds good" comment from peer reviewers during workshops, which indicates the reviewers' approval. But most times, the "sounds good" comment is of little use—other than to protect the feelings of the author. It is helpful to encourage students to entirely avoid the "sounds good" comment, or, if they use it, to attach it to some concrete description of what was in fact done well.

I tell students that the "sounds good" comment can never stand alone; they must be able to articulate *precisely* what was done well. Of course there are times when writing doesn't sound good and when reviewers are reluctant to share their criticism. In these cases, it is important to stress the constructive dynamic of criticism rather than criticism itself. Instead of saying "this sounds really bad" or "I don't like what you've done here," reviewers should be encouraged to articulate what exactly they didn't like and, if possible, a way to make it better. Practicing constructive criticism in this way is important to ensure that peer review offers concrete feedback rather than vague commentary. Table 5 offers examples for constructive criticism in peer review.

As the model in figure 27 shows, assigning virtual peer review requires planning. It is not an intuitive activity for students, and consequently instructors should spend some time helping students become comfortable with the activity. While the model I propose is an example of implementing virtual peer review, it can be easily adapted to different technologies and peer review goals.

Evaluating Student Writing Using Virtual Peer Review

If instructors require students to complete peer review virtually (and especially if course objectives reflect technological literacy), instructors might consider

Table 5
Making Peer Review Criticism Constructive

Vague, Unhelpful Criticism	*Specific, Constructive Criticism*
"This introduction doesn't make sense."	"I don't have a clear idea from your introduction what the main idea of your paper is. Can you make it more clear?"
"I don't like the illustration you used in this paragraph."	"The illustration in paragraph 5 doesn't seem to fit with the topic sentence of that paragraph. Is there an example you could include that makes the point more strongly?"
"This sounds bad."	"This sentence doesn't work for me because your language is very informal. You might consider how to restate this sentence in a more formal way."
"These paragraphs don't seem to flow well."	"Paragraph 2 doesn't set up the idea you discuss in paragraph 3 very well. Consider reorganizing these paragraphs or insert a transition between them."

conducting virtual peer review themselves as they evaluate student writing (similar to the scenario of evaluation I described in chapter 5). Evaluating student writing through virtual peer review requires students to turn in their assignments to instructors electronically, and there are several ways this task could be accomplished. One is that students could place their writing in a "drop box"—an electronic folder in which students can place their writing, but cannot retrieve it. (Drop boxes are a common feature in several Web courseware packages.) Using the drop box method, instructors could read student writing and provide feedback either intertextually using word processing or via endnotes in asynchronous messages. Another way students could submit writing electronically is by turning in their work on a diskette; the instructor could then read it, provide comments, and create a new (saved) document with instructor comments (the diskette would be returned to the student). Furthermore, if instructors wanted to "chat" with students about their work, they could set up conference times using a synchronous chat tool and meet virtually to discuss student writing.

There are several reasons why evaluating student writing virtually may benefit students. First, having instructors respond to student writing using computer technology would immediately reinforce the value of virtual peer review. Although students may not be asked to *evaluate* other student writing per se (recall the various scenarios for virtual peer review I discussed in chapter 5), students would get the sense that instructors "practice what they preach." That is, students can see ways in which instructors use various technological tools to provide response to an author's writing. Second, when instructors provide comments either asynchronously (intertextually or through endnotes) or synchronously (through online chats), they can also get a sense of how the technological tools are working for students. If, for example, instructors use the same synchronous and asynchronous tools that students are required to use for virtual peer review, they can more concretely understand advantages and disadvantages of those tools; they can experience firsthand the satisfaction or frustrations certain tools afford. Such experience can go a long way toward helping students adapt to virtual peer review.

Third, evaluating student writing online allows instructors the opportunity to observe how technology shapes their response to student writing. For example, instructors may find they offer *more* feedback virtually and spend *more* time evaluating student writing; they may experience ways that roles of reader and author converge in virtual space; and they may develop efficient systems for providing comments on student writing. And, since responding to writing is so much a part of the life of an academic (reviewing scholarship of others; receiving comments on their own writing; collaborating with colleagues on various documents), the experience instructors can gain through online evaluation may benefit instructors professionally.

Online Writing Centers

Virtual peer review has concrete implications for another area of writing studies: online writing centers. As I mentioned in chapter 1, online writing centers, also known as "Online Writing Labs" or OWLs, are academic tutoring services designed especially for writing support. Although most OWLs have been created as counterparts to face-to-face writing centers, some exist only online (Shadle 8). However, technology has been integrated into OWLs in drastically different ways. For example, as Jane Lasarenko reports, some centers use computer technology only to advertise their services on the Web; some—like Purdue's well-known OWL—use the Web to provide online resources and handouts about writing; and some use Internet technologies for asynchronous or synchronous tutoring. Online writing centers are not created equally and vary significantly in terms of their uses of technology.

Not surprisingly, like writing studies, online writing centers have been rife with struggle over how (and whether) to integrate computer technology. Although there has been a surge of scholarship on online writing centers in recent years (evidenced in works like *Wiring the Writing Center* and *Taking Flight with OWLs*), many scholars have expressed skepticism about introducing technology into writing centers. Reasons for resisting technology in writing centers ranges from lack of funding or resources to strong beliefs that online writing center tutoring *cannot* be as useful as face-to-face tutoring (Shadle 5). In addition, as Joanna Castner reports, in light of the strong dialogic tradition in face-to-face tutoring, some technologies do not appear capable of sustaining ongoing feedback and dialogue for students. Indeed, some have expressed fears that online writing centers revive the "fix-it shop" reputation that writing center scholars have worked so hard to overcome (Castner 127). And, as Randall Beebe and Mary Bonevelle suggest, the induction of technology into writing centers seems to further complicate the theory/practice dichotomy that already exists in writing center work (42).

However, as many scholars have noted, online writing centers can be successful when they *shape technology to specific pedagogical purposes*. As Beebe and Bonevelle put it:

> Integrating technology effectively into writing centers demands a thorough and honest rethinking of where and how the gap between theory and practice most sharply affects any given writing center. Although difficult, such rethinking can push writing centers both to determine what they most want to retain as they integrate technology and to clarify—perhaps enhance—their role in educational institutions. (42)

As we seek ways to maximize the benefits of technology for writing centers, virtual peer review can offer useful contributions, and can even contribute to a rethinking of writing centers of the sort that Beebe and Bonevelle describe. To begin, virtual peer review highlights the ways technology can be used to support *tutoring activity* rather than peripheral aspects of writing centers such as online resources or visual images. For example, some online writing centers emulate a physical space, using pictures or images of couches, steaming cups of coffee, or even audio of people chatting to one another. I argue that creating online writing centers in terms of environment or physical spaces may not be as effective as creating them for specific activities and purposes—in this case, tutoring activity. When adopting virtual peer review, online writing centers may encourage tutors and students alike to associate technology with writing and tutoring activities.

In addition, virtual peer review can be supported by pedagogical goals and assumptions associated with writing pedagogy (writing as a process; writing as a social act; student-centered writing instruction), thus actualizing the guideline that *pedagogy must drive technology*. This pedagogical grounding of virtual peer review, as well as the careful planning necessary to complete it, may dissipate skepticism about the integration of technology into writing centers.

Finally, integrating virtual peer review into writing centers offers students another avenue for receiving tutoring assistance. Some students appreciate the convenience afforded by virtual peer review, especially in cases where schedules or distance prevent a student from visiting a writing center in person. In addition, virtual peer review increases options for assistance, because it can be enacted using a range of technologies. Tutors might practice virtual peer review through asynchronous, intertextual exchange with students (e-mail or word processing), or they may meet with students online to chat about their writing. These options may allow tutors to reach out to students who may not otherwise visit a writing center in person.

To illustrate what an online writing center redesigned around virtual peer review might look like, I can offer an account of the Online Writing Center at University of Minnesota, where I have had the opportunity to participate in directing and shaping the mission of the service.[1] Rather than broadening tutor services to include workshops and extensive resources, or to concentrate on emulating a physical space through the image of doors on the home page, the most recent revision of the Online Writing Center is based on virtual peer review as the primary activity of the center. In this version of the Online Writing Center, tutoring happens only asynchronously, but within these sessions tutors provide detailed intertextual and summary comments for students—in a sense, students receive a thorough peer review from tutors. Asynchronous tutoring is facilitated through document exchange on the Web site, and tutors record comments electronically through word-processing tools such as "comment" functions and footnotes (see figure 28).[2] Although the level of simultaneous dialogue between student and tutor is diminished due to asynchronous exchanges, certainly the level of interaction with text and ideas is elevated. Tutors in this center do not "fix" or edit papers, but through electronic comments tutors ask questions and offer suggestions for revision based on requests the students make when they submit their writing for review.

One advantage of focusing the Online Writing Center on the activity of virtual peer review has been a clarification of its purpose and mission. As I have mentioned before, the Online Writing Center exists only online; there is no face-to-face center to accompany it. This lack of physical presence has caused some confusion among instructors and students who cannot "locate" the service. We discovered that focusing tutoring services on the single activity of virtual peer review has helped people better understand the primary service of the center. This focus has also affected the expectations students and instructors have of the service; students know they will receive a thorough peer review of their work, and they are free to contact tutors to continue the discussion. Although this Online Writing Center only represents an asynchronous version of virtual peer review, virtual peer review could also be conducted synchronously in online writing centers, and many scholars have reported their preference for this approach because it most closely resembles face-to-face

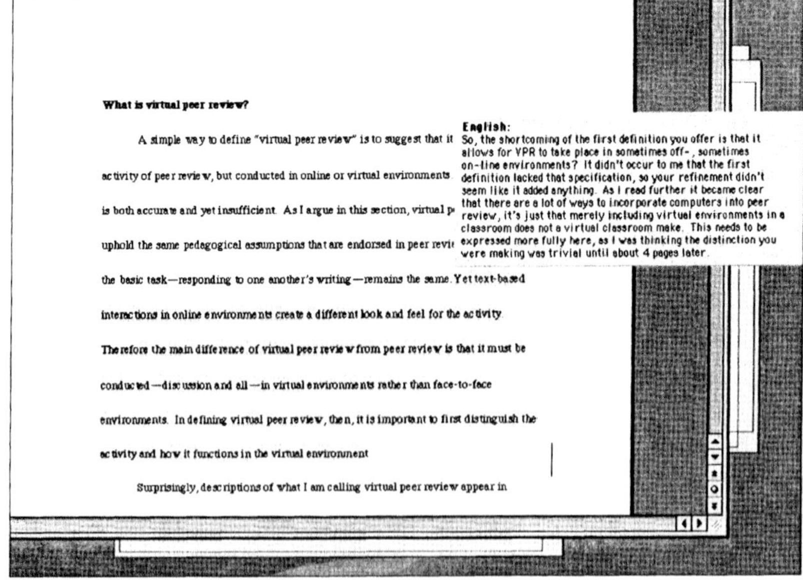

Figure 28. Virtual Peer Review in the Online Writing Center

tutoring (Crump). The point is that when a clear purpose for online writing centers has been identified, the implementation of technology becomes easier to grasp. Truly, virtual peer review can be a key activity that drives online writing center work.

Writing-Across-the-Curriculum

Virtual peer review also has implications for writing-across-the-curriculum (WAC) movements. Before discussing the contributions of virtual peer review to this context, I must provide some background about WAC and discuss why it is an appropriate context for virtual peer review.

As David R. Russell explains in *Writing in the Academic Disciplines,* WAC began appearing in the 1970s as a response to the lagging performance among students in general composition courses (8).[3] Instead of relegating writing instruction to composition instructors, WAC movements assert that *all* instructors have a responsibility to participate in writing instruction. Furthermore, some have argued that when writing is integrated into disciplinary contexts—rather than isolated in composition courses—students have a stronger appreciation for writing and better understand how it applies to their professional interests. WAC programs also promote the value of writing in the process of learning (Herrington).

Since the 1970s, WAC programs have become well established in many colleges and universities across the nation. Although programs may vary from one to the next, a common characteristic of WAC programs is that they supplement course credit with a designated writing-intensive credit. Each university stipulates how this credit is to be earned, but typically this writing-intensive credit requires a certain number of written pages per course as well as the opportunity for students to revise at least one assignment. Thus, when a course takes on an additional writing-intensive credit, instructors of those courses also take on the task of integrating writing into their courses in new ways, and often they request help from composition faculty (or established writing services). Consequently, a large body of scholarship exists that describes writing-intensive assignments that can be integrated into disciplines such as biology, chemistry, physics, math, psychology, sociology, and agriculture. In addition, WAC scholars have begun to explore the ways writing *technologies* can be integrated across the disciplines, as the book *Electronic Communication across the Curriculum* demonstrates. Some suggestions for integrating technology include using e-mail for class discussions, creating Web sites and Web assignments for students, integrating computer-supported collaborative assignments, and conducting student-teacher conferencing (Reiss, Selfe, and Young).

Like composition, WAC is a field that values diversity of instructional approaches. Virtual peer review has the potential to contribute to WAC programs, because it encourages revision and can easily supplement writing-intensive courses. (The case study I reviewed in chapter 4 is an example of how virtual peer review was integrated into a writing-intensive course.) In fact, there are many benefits to integrating virtual peer review into writing-intensive courses. One is the inherent emphasis of virtual peer review on revision; revision is often a requirement of writing-intensive courses, and virtual peer review is a logical way to meet this requirement. As such, virtual peer review presents a unified approach to addressing writing in discipline-specific courses, for its consistent practice reinforces the importance of revision in these courses perhaps more completely than awkward or isolated writing assignments that have been squeezed into an already full curriculum.

Another benefit of virtual peer review in writing-intensive courses is the simultaneous integration of technology with writing. Some faculty may be interested in opportunities to strengthen both writing and technology in their classes, and certainly virtual peer review would address this goal. Indeed, the case to implement writing with technology may be made more easily among faculty members outside of composition than within it, especially among those for whom technological literacy is important to their discipline. Consider, for example, the CPR™ program that I reviewed in chapters 1 and 5, in which the developers of the program acknowledged the role of both technology and peer review in scientific writing. Virtual peer review is an efficient and useful way to integrate technology and writing emphases. Clearly though, when integrating virtual peer review in writing-intensive courses, instructors must survey their options for technology. Does the course have access to a computer lab? Does the course already have a Web presence? Are instructors using programs like WebCT or Blackboard? CPR™? Do students in the class have access to technologies such as word processing and e-mail? Instructors must address these questions if they expect students to effectively integrate virtual peer review.

A third benefit of virtual peer review for writing-intensive courses is that the activity can be conducted outside of class. Having consulted with WAC faculty for several years, I have discovered that a common concern among writing-intensive instructors is taking class time for activities like peer review or spending too much time on writing rather than on course content. This concern presents its own challenges, such as reminding faculty that writing is not easily separated from "content" and thus is best presented as an integral part of learning. However, time remains a concern among faculty when planning writing-intensive courses. Virtual peer review offers a useful alternative in these cases, because it can be conducted outside of class. The trade-off, however, is that instructors must prepare students for virtual peer review; as I mentioned, I encourage writing-intensive faculty to spend at least one class period focused on peer review and virtual forms of peer review. The suggestions provided in figure 27 apply as well to writing-across-the-curriculum and can be adapted as necessary.

To illustrate how virtual peer review can be integrated into a writing-intensive course, it is worth commenting on the agronomy/animal science course I discussed in chapter 4. For this course, many of the steps in figure 27 were implemented; for example, students were given background and training on peer review, instructors assigned long-term groups, and instructors also created online spaces for each group in a program called WebBoard that facilitated synchronous and asynchronous discussions. The first peer review session, held early in the semester, was conducted in class in a face-to-face environment. All other peer review sessions were conducted outside of class using WebBoard.

In this case, the most interesting result was that despite laborious efforts of instructors to set up virtual peer review technologies for the class, the majority of students tended to complete peer reviews by hand rather than through the WebBoard technology. This finding is a strong indication that preparation for virtual peer review is more important than we might think. As I discussed in chapter 4, the students who *did* try virtual peer review (24 percent of all students) tended to use their own e-mail accounts rather than WebBoard technology, because they found e-mail faster and more convenient than using WebBoard.[4] These findings suggests that, when left to their own devices, students will find the easiest, most comfortable route. If instructors really want students to use a specific technology they have selected, they should test and retest the technology to ensure its usability, and they should firmly encourage students to try the technology they have selected. Not coincidentally, in hindsight, instructors of the agronomy/animal science course thought even *more* class time should be spent preparing students for virtual peer review and reminding them of the technologies available to them. They were right.

In terms of writing-across-the-curriculum, then, virtual peer review has potential for writing-intensive courses, but it must be carefully planned and consistently integrated. Virtual peer review is an activity that makes sense when instructors desire to incorporate both technology and writing in their classrooms, and when they thoroughly prepare for the activity.

Workplace Writing

As I discussed in chapter 1, virtual peer review is already occurring in workplace writing, in areas such as technical communication, editing, and collaborative writing. That virtual peer review is appearing in these contexts is not surprising. In recent years, technology in workplace communication has received frequent attention, especially among scholars in technical and professional communication. For example, Shoshana Zuboff explains in *In the Age of the Smart Machine* that introducing technology in workplace environments brings with it a complicated web of issues related to organizational structures, work satisfaction, and work habits (389). Likewise, Jennie Dautermann reports that when technology is introduced in workplace environments, it has the potential to influence work patterns and power structures (21). Scholars have examined the role of technology in workplace contexts, observing aspects such as social theories of language (Duin and Hansen); contextual analyses (Sims; Henderson); the use of specific technologies such as databases, hypertext, and online editing tools (Mirel; Farkas and Poltrock); and gaps between workplace and academic uses of technology (Selber; Hansen).

Situated among the many uses of technologies in workplace environments, virtual peer review most closely resembles activities such as online revising and editing. For example, colleagues may review a document and provide feedback at various stages. Using tools such as "track changes," they may select a graphical option (underline, color, or highlight) to distinguish their comments from those of other reviewers. As I mentioned in chapter 1, models of "online editing" have been shared in technical communication scholarship (Farkas and Poltrock; Sims; "Professional Counseling Journals"). Certainly, virtual peer review can become a central activity for editors of academic journals and editors in workplace environments. Not only does virtual peer review integrate technology into writing practices, but it reduces costs associated with publishing, such as copying and mailing print drafts to reviewers.

In addition to online revising and editing, virtual peer review can be a part of collaborative writing in the workplace. Indeed, collaborative writing practices offer ample opportunities to practice virtual peer review, not only asynchronously, but also synchronously. Collaborative software packages, for instance, allow team members to meet synchronously to discuss a project, while viewing a draft of a document shown on the screen. Asynchronously, team members may use groupware or simple e-mail to communicate back and forth about changes to documents. Options for virtual peer review in workplaces abound as collaborative software continues to advance. And opportunities for virtual peer review in workplaces will most likely continue to rise because of the frequency of collaboration in workplace settings. As Rebecca Burnett reports, as much as 75 to 85 percent of workplace writing may involve collaboration (*Technical Communication* 131).

As opportunities for virtual peer review in workplace writing arise, however, we must be mindful of the complexities that are likely to emerge. Just as challenges emerge in classrooms, there are likely to be challenges facing workplace environments. For example, what if a team member uses one method of response, and another team member chooses a different method? What if, over the course of one week, team members comment on a document at least three or four times? What if no one on the team is managing the review process? What if versions of the document become blurred, and it becomes *more* work to iron out the latest iteration? What if colleagues have different comfort levels and attitudes about technology? What if international colleagues introduce issues of translation, cultural expectations, or software compatibility? What if timelines and schedules are not coordinated?

Considering all the potential complexities that may arise, it is important to remember that virtual peer review is not necessarily a quick fix to collaborative writing situations and does not guarantee increased efficiency. It is true that virtual peer review enhances the speed with which review processes can be done—at least initially. That is, authors can send their writing more quickly via the Internet than via "snail mail," but such speed does not guarantee that a reviewer might respond as quickly. (A reviewer might take just as long to return comments using e-mail as using snail mail.) The real advantage of virtual peer review for workplace writing is the efficiency with which writing can be *delivered* across distance, and the speed with which delivery can be handled. Reviewers still bear the burden, however, of meeting deadlines for response imposed by coworkers or superiors. But if colleagues have not planned the activity, frustrations are likely to arise. Efficiency in virtual peer review comes only when those participating in the activity plan their approach in advance, considering their goals and selecting technology appropriate to those goals. Understanding this reality goes a long way toward making virtual peer review more efficient.

Perhaps, then, the greatest challenge facing writers in the workplace is *project management*—coordinating group goals, schedules, and methods for feedback and revision. With multiple drafts and instances of feedback, it is most helpful if a team member is designated to manage the revision process—to summarize the feedback from reviewers, to coordinate revision schedules, and to facilitate decision-making processes regarding final revisions. It is also helpful if the team engages in a planning process for using virtual peer review, considering goals for virtual peer review before launching into the activity. Such a process need not take much time, and could even be proposed by a team leader. Here again, Burnett and Clark's suggestions for use of collaborative technologies may be useful: one should consider the group characteristics, group agreements, task characteristics, and technology environment. Table 3 in chapter 4 suggests a range of options for conducting virtual peer review, given these factors. To increase efficiency, workplace teams might routinely complete a simple form that forces them to articulate those factors. Such a form is shown in figure 29. This form could be used as a cover sheet for projects involving virtual peer review. Ideally, this form would be completed by the project leader after the team has reached group agreements about the task and technologies accessible to all members. For example, under "Task Instructions," the team leader could specify different stages of the review process. Task 1 might require all members to contribute detailed, intertextual comments using word processing; then members would send their comments via e-mail attachment to the team leader by a specified date and time. Task 2 might require all members to participate in a synchronous chat about the document, using a program that accommodates split-screen windows for viewing the document and chatting simultaneously. Task 3 might require only two team members to conduct thorough proofreading using a "track changes" tool, to be returned to the team leader via e-mail attachment by a specified date and time. As a cover sheet, then, this form simply reminds group members of decisions about deadlines, member responsibilities, tasks, and methods of virtual peer review response; it could be a timesaving device, especially when projects involve multiple reviewers.

In sum, virtual peer review is likely to be a frequent workplace activity in terms of editing, revising, and collaborating. Drawing attention to virtual peer review as a distinct writing activity may assist workplace writers in facilitating this activity, and engaging in some kind of planning process is likely to empower writers and reduce any potential frustrations that arise.

Future Research and Directions

As this chapter demonstrates, virtual peer review not only provides insight into issues about computer pedagogy but also holds potential for several writing contexts. Although this potential is exciting, it produces many questions about virtual peer review to consider for further examination. Such questions may include:

- In what ways does virtual peer review influence student writing performance?
- In what ways does virtual peer review encourage quality of response?
- How well does virtual peer review establish the connection between pedagogical purpose and technology uses?
- What connections exist between student written response and instructor written response?
- How often is virtual peer review used in workplace writing and what benefits and drawbacks arise as a result?
- Over a long-range period, how might attitudes of instructors and students change regarding virtual peer review in comparison with face-to-face peer review?

Title of Project/Job Number:		Start Date:	Completion Date:
Project Leader:		Contact Information:	

Team Members	Role/Title	Contact Information	Special Concerns (Schedules, language, etc.)
1.			
2.			
3.			
4.			
5.			
6.			

Task Instructions	Technology Specifications	Group Members Responsible	Completion Date
1.			
2.			
3.			
4.			
Technological Support Person:		Contact Information:	

Figure 29. Project Worksheet for Incorporating Virtual Peer Review in the Workplace

These questions are worthy of continued research and examination. My purpose has been to draw attention to virtual peer review, define it more fully, and discuss its potential as a pedagogical activity. Clearly, further research needs to be done to determine the usefulness of virtual peer review in context and to begin to better understand how technology can be integrated into the activity of providing feedback about writing.

Conclusion

The purpose of this book has been to acknowledge the ways peer review may change when computer technology is employed, and to begin investigating the implications of *virtual peer review* for writing studies. I contend that virtual peer review is a remediation of peer review in the sense that computer technology introduces important differences, such as the primacy of written communication and new challenges associated with collaboration and technology. In describing virtual peer review, I have argued that the activity reflects the well-established guideline that *pedagogy must drive technology;* that attitudes about extending peer review to virtual environments are complex; and that virtual peer review is most effective when writers take control of technology. I have also suggested that virtual peer review can be applied broadly to several writing contexts; as such, it holds great promise for the field of computers and writing.

However, adapting peer review to virtual environments is not a passive event. It requires that we think strategically about the technology before us and that we shape technology to our writing purposes. As such, virtual peer review is an act of technological literacy, for it requires critical thinking about technology in terms of goals to be accomplished and our uses of technologies to facilitate those goals. Thus, I argue that virtual peer review has implications for writing studies that go beyond implications of face-to-face peer review. In addition to supporting social construction and the ways writers interact about scholarship, virtual peer review supports *technological literacy* in writing studies. Virtual peer review has the potential to become a cornerstone for computer-based writing instruction, for it is solidly grounded in writing studies and fully aware of computer technology in writing practice.

As I close, I would like to suggest that we have much more to learn about virtual peer review; I have merely opened the floor to discussion on the subject. Virtual peer review offers a unique opportunity to observe how writing is active, for virtual peer review involves reading, writing, and interacting, and can be productively managed in virtual environments. Virtual peer review also offers us the opportunity to examine forms of peer written response and to examine the usefulness of those forms of response. Finally, virtual peer review raises the question of whether or not quality of response substantially improves when peer review is conducted via computer technology. Perhaps these avenues will be explored and shared in future research.

Peer Review and Technology Instructions

Peer Review: A Technique for Improving Writing

What is peer review?

Peer review is an exercise in which students review each other's written work. Peer review is often connected to revision-a part of the writing process in which writers refine and make substantive changes to their written work.

To conduct peer review, students simply exchange written work with other students, read the work, and provide comments to help the author improve. The benefits of peer review are that students can see how others have approached their work, and they can practice being part of a writing community.

Why conduct peer review?

Receiving constructive feedback from peers is a vital activity for workplace writers. Written communication that includes technical or scientific information should be checked for accuracy, expression, appropriate address of audience and purpose, and adequate support. Peer review is often conducted in the workplace among technical writers.

How can I participate in peer review?

Peer review can be conducted in paired student groups. Each student exchanges her paper with her partner. The two students can then read each others' papers and discuss places where the papers could be improved. Worksheets to guide peer review could also be included in these pair peer reviews. Generally peer review in pairs can be completed in one class period.

What do you need to know about peer review?

Before conducting peer review, you need to understand:

1. **Roles of reviewers**

2. **Appropriate dialogue strategies**

3. **Suggestions for constructive criticism.**

1. Roles in Peer Review

A peer review may consist of two or more persons, but generally, there are two roles in peer review: that of the author or writer, and that of the reviewer.

The role of the person whose writing is being reviewed is that of the **author**. During the peer review, the author may be asked questions by the reviewer. The author might take the opportunity to discuss ideas for revision with the reviewer.

The role of the person or persons reading the paper is that of the **reviewer**. The reviewer will take time during the peer review to read through the author's paper, and then will ask questions of the author for further clarification. The reviewer should feel free to point out areas that need improvement as well as areas that are done particularly well. The reviewer's role is to constructively provide feedback from a reader's point of view.

During a peer review, participants will switch roles, so that everyone gets a chance to be the author whose work is reviewed and everyone gets a chance to be a reviewer. Peer review should be a positive experience, and it is helpful if the persons involved approach peer review with a positive outcome in mind. It is easy to fear the response of others, but both author and reviewer should keep in mind that reviewing each other's work is a fruitful, constructive experience. Approaching roles positively in a peer review is key to a good peer review experience.

2. Avoid the "Sounds Good" Comment: Appropriate Dialogue Strategies

It is tempting for reviewers to fall into the trap of commenting "Sounds good." Instead of providing constructive feedback, reviewers might simply tell the author, "Your paper sounds good. Everything seems to be in place.

Good job!" Merely commenting "'sounds good" does little to help an author with the process of revision. Reviewers should be prepared to provide positive comments that help the student improve his or her writing.

We encourage peer reviews to be an opportunity for active dialogue. During a peer review, the **reviewer** might ask questions of the **author** for clarification on the paper. Questions could be about content, context, audience, purpose, organization, support, design, or expression. In answering any questions the reviewer asks, the author should take the opportunity to discuss his or her paper in detail. To help the reviewer ask constructive questions, we offer the following list of questions for the reviewer (found in table 1).

3. Suggestions for Constructive Criticism

A reviewer may often feel awkward making comments about another student's paper, particularly if the reviewer finds something that needs to be improved. However, peer reviews are not productive if the reviewer only provides positive comments. It is important that the peer reviewer feel comfortable in offering his or her perspective about trouble spots in an author's paper, but we advocate doing this gently. Reviewers should keep in mind that peer review is the opportunity to provide constructive criticism, not negative feedback.

To achieve constructive criticism, it is helpful if the reviewer phrases his or her comments in terms of "I" statements to address trouble spots in an author's paper. The reviewer might follow up with a question to help the author articulate his or her intention in the paper. The examples in table 2 show original negative statements and ways those statements might be revised to demonstrate constructive criticism.

Sample Transcript: Version 1

R = Reviewer
A = Author

R: OK, I've completed the worksheet and now we should probably discuss your paper for a few minutes.

A: OK.

R: Basically, I didn't find anything huge or big that needed to be changed.

Table 1

Sample Questions the Reviewer Can Ask the Author

Content	Tell me about the technical or scientific content in your paper.
	What terms or definitions are important to your paper?
	In what ways do you use these terms or definitions?
	What other technical information is important to your paper?
Context	What are the requirements for this assignment according to the instructor's assignment sheet?
	What sections do you still need to work on or include?
Audience	Who is the primary audience for your paper?
	Are there any other persons that will read this paper?
	What does the target audience want to learn from your paper?
	What language, visuals, or information do you need to include to target this audience?
Purpose	What purpose are you trying to convey most strongly in this paper (to inform, persuade, instruct)?
	Do you think you have communicated this purpose adequately in your paper? If so, how?
Organization	What was your plan for organizing this paper?
	How do the sections, headings, and subheadings work together?
	What do you have left to do on organization?
Support	What kinds of support have you included in this paper in terms of sources, illustrations, or examples?
	Do you have plans to include more support for the paper?
	If so, where and what would you include?
	What style of documentation are you using? Have you included internal and external citations correctly?
Design	What word-processing program did you use for your paper?
	Does it include margins, font, and spacing appropriate to this assignment?
	Is your paper neat and easy to read visually?
	What figures, charts, or visual illustrations have you included?
Expression	Are there any trouble spots you know of with grammar, punctuation, or spelling?
	Have you used an appropriate tone (professional? personal? academic?) for the assignment?
	Have you used an appropriate register (informal vs. formal)?
	Are there any specific terms you have not included?

Table 2

Negative Comments Transformed to Constructive Criticism Using "I" Statements

Negative Comment	*Constructive Criticism*
"Your paragraph on the history of Turf-grass industry doesn't make sense."	"I am having trouble understanding your paragraph on the history of Turf-grass industry. Can you tell me what you are trying to convey in this paragraph?"
"You haven't addressed audience at all in your letter of transmittal."	"I do not get a strong sense of audience in your letter of transmittal. Can you tell me whom you are trying to address?"
"This section is really poorly organized."	"I don't understand the organization of this section. Can you explain what you are trying to do here?"
"This figure in your lab report is not clear. It looks terrible."	"I'm having a hard time seeing how this figure fits in with your lab report. What does this figure address? Where is the title of this figure? As a reader, it would be helpful to me to have labels and a clear title for this figure so I can understand what you want to illustrate with this figure."

A: Really? I thought there were a few sections that were confusing.

R: Like which ones?

A: My introduction that discusses literature about my topic. I didn't know if I had included the sources correctly there or not.

R: Oh, yeah, that was where you referred to two sources.

A: Yes.

R: Well, I thought that was OK. I mean, we don't need to do anything too elaborate, just so we refer to the source, I guess. I thought it was fine.

A: Well, did you understand the introduction?

R: Yeah, I thought, um, basically you were saying . . . um, let me see here. (Reads through introduction quickly.) Yeah, that was OK. Your sources address one aspect of your topic, but isn't your paper about the other aspect of your topic? I guess it's alright what you've done here. Yeah, I get it just fine.

Questions for Discussion

In what ways was this dialogue productive? If not, why not?

What constructive feedback did the reviewer provide the author? Explain.

What areas were addressed in this dialogue: content, context, audience, purpose, organization, support, design, or expression?

Sample Transcript: Version 2

R = Reviewer
A = Author

R: OK, I've completed the worksheet and now we should probably discuss your paper for a few minutes.

A: OK. Where do you want to start?

R: Let's start with the introduction. One of the questions on the worksheet talks about documenting sources.

A: Yeah. I included two sources in my introduction.

R: Yes, but I was wondering why you chose those sources? It was hard for me to tell how they introduced your topic. They didn't address the subject of your paper. Can you tell me what you were trying to do here?

A: I was trying to introduce the opposite viewpoint, you know, to set the stage for my topic, so that I would introduce the point of view that I thought was best. I was trying to contrast the two viewpoints.

R: I was thinking that it might help to include one source that backs up your viewpoint. Then it would be easier for me to see what your main topic was.

A: Ok, that's a good idea. Thanks.

R: Also, did you include your sources on a bibliography? I didn't see them on your bibliography.

A: OK, so I should add the intro sources to the bibliography?

R: Yeah, I think that is what we are supposed to do.

Questions for Discussion

In what ways was this dialogue productive? If not, why not?

What constructive feedback did the reviewer provide the author? Explain.

Did the reviewer's comments come across as constructive or negative? What dialogue strategies did the reviewer use?

These materials were written by Dr. Lee-Ann Kastman, Department of Rhetoric, University of Minnesota. For more information on this topic, contact Dr. Kastman at +1 612 624 6727 or kastm001@tc.umn.edu
College of Agricultural, Food & Environmental Sciences
Department of Rhetoric

This page last modified 25-Oct-99 by Lee-Ann Kastman
URL=http:llwww.agricola.umn.edu/owc/WritingIntensive

WebBoard Instructions
General Information

1. WebBoard is located at http://hal9000.rhetoric.umn.edu:6070/ ~AnSc3203.

2. When you arrive at the site, you will enter as an "Existing User" (we have already entered you into the system, so you are not a "new user"): In the Name field, enter your X500 name (such as raci0109), and in the Password field, enter your student ID#. Click Log In

3. The next screen you see will list "Conferences" on the left and a Welcome! screen on the right. Conferences for your class will include Welcome, Instructions, General Comments, and your group's private conference. Anyone can contribute to the first three conferences, but only members of your group can contribute to their group conference. In fact, you will only see your group conference listed.

4. If there is a plus sign in front of the conference name, that means there are messages posted within that conference. The number in the parenthesis indicates the number of messages in that conference. For example,

+ General Comments (7)

indicates that there are subtopics available under the conference "General Comments," and that there are seven total messages in the General Comments conference.

5. To view messages, click on the plus sign. Below the conference title will appear a listing of message topics. Click on the topic you want to see, and on the right side of the screen, the messages will appear.

6. As with the conferences, if there are multiple messages (a thread) under a topic, a plus sign will appear in front of the topic name. You can scroll the right screen in order to view all the messages posted within a topic.

Using WebBoard

There are four main commands involved with using the WebBoard: **Post, Reply, Edit,** and **Delete.** These commands can be accessed from the menu bar on the right side of the screen that appears after you have chosen a conference topic.

Post

Use **Post** to start conversations, such as "Our Schedule for Project One" or "Unresolved Issues for Project One." The **Post** command can be accessed from three areas:

- the main menu bar visible at all times at the top of the screen:

- the submenu bar visible when viewing a post:

**Post | Reply | Reply/Quote | Email Reply | Delete | Edit
Previous | Next | Previous Topic | Next Topic | Entire Topic**

- or, as a text link on the bottom of the right screen, below each message and under the rule line.

Post New Topic | Reply to: "<Message Name>"

Once you have finished writing your message, click the **Post** button. WebBoard will spellcheck your message. Use your browser's back button to correct any misspelled words. When you are satisfied with your message, click **Post** again.

<u>Reply</u>

Use the **Reply** command to send a response to the message currently on the right screen. As with the **Post** command, **Reply** can be accessed from two areas. You may reply to a post in three ways:

- To reply to a message, choose "Reply."

- If you wish to include the text of the original message, choose **"Reply/Quote."**

- If you would like to send a private reply to the individual, select **"Email Reply"** and the message will be sent to his or her e-mail account, and will not be present on your WebBoard.

<u>Edit and Delete</u>

At any time you can choose to **Edit** or **Delete** previously posted messages; just make sure the message you want to work with is displayed on the right side of the screen

Navigation Tools

While the top line of the submenu bar provides the tool options for conversing, the bottom line provides navigation.

Post | Reply | Reply/Quote | Email Reply | Delete | Edit
Previous | Next | Previous Topic | Next Topic | Entire Topic

———————➤

This section of the submenu bar is self-explanatory. You should note that **"Previous"** and **"Next"** refer to messages, not topics, as the last three commands do.

That's all, folks. We've made WebBoard available to you because groups have had much success in using the software to support their groups. Give it a healthy test drive, and we're sure you'll like it.

APPENDIX **B**

Consent Form

Title of Study: Exploring a "Dialogic Pedagogy"
in Distance Educational Environments

You are invited to be in a research study that will closely examine the ways that instructors use dialogues mediated by technology such as ITV class discussions, e-mail, and Web chats. You have been identified as a possible participant because you have enrolled for a course that includes electronic or ITV dialogues, you are instructing the course, or you are involved in the electronic tutoring of students studying writing. I ask that you consider this research opportunity and ask any questions you may have before agreeing to be in the study.

This study is being conducted by the University of Minnesota.

Background Information

The purpose of this study is to better understand the use of technological dialogues as a teaching strategy in distance courses.

Procedures

If you agree to be in this study, I would ask you to complete two surveys, allow me access to your online discussions, and possibly participate in an interview about your experience. Your participation will not exceed four hours of your time over the course of the semester.

Risks and Benefits

There are no foreseeable risks associated with your participation in this study. Participation in this study may benefit you by increasing your awareness of technology used in courses that incorporate dialogues. Your participation will also help instructors at the University of Minnesota learn more about the effectiveness of technologies used for distance education.

159

Voluntary Nature of the Study

Your participation is strictly voluntary, and you are not required to participate in this study. You can withdraw from the study at any time. Your grade will not be affected in any way, whether or not you participate in this study.

Confidentiality

The records of this study will be kept private. In any sort of report I might publish, I will not include any information that will make it possible to identify a subject. If you desire, pseudonyms will be used in place of your real name to protect your identity. If you agree to participate in interviews, your interviews will be recorded (either on audio- or videotape). Only I will have access to the data, and the data will be stored for only one year.

Contacts and Questions

The researcher conducting this study is Dr. Lee-Ann Kastman Breuch. You may ask any questions you have about the study now. If you have questions later, you may contact me through e-mail (kastm001@tc.umn.edu) or phone: (612) 624-6727. You will be given a copy of this form to keep for your files.

Statement of Consent

I have read the above information. I have asked questions and have received answers to my questions. I consent to participate in the study.

Signature ____________________________________ **Date** ________

Signature of Investigator _______________________ **Date** ________

Notes

Chapter One

1. I note that even the virtual peer review I just described was not originally discussed in terms of peer review but rather in terms of computer pedagogy.

Chapter Three

1. However, Bruffee is also suggesting that the term "conversation" applies to writing as well as speech, although he notes the differences of time and space.

2. Rorty suggests that "kooky" would classify abnormal discourse that is truly odd and perhaps nonsensical; thus, ineffectual. He uses the term "revolutionary" to classify abnormal discourse that is persuasive and useful, and powerful enough to effect change of the normal discourse.

Chapter Four

1. All students and instructors granted permission to use excerpts from online dialogues, provided that anonymity was protected. For a copy of the consent form, see appendix B.

Chapter Five

1. Ken Kastman discusses this concept in relation to reviewing written documents of engineers.

2. Note that by this intertextuality I do not mean to suggest that virtual peer reviewers actively coauthor texts; rather, they become author of their own comments in which they articulate feedback for the author.

3. Saving is a CRITICAL step, because if virtual peer reviewers do not save their comments, they are immediately lost and reviewers must start the process over again. I encourage students to save their comments by conducting a "save as" (command in

word-processing programs). When labeling the document, I encourage them to put their initials in the title of the document (e.g., Paper1.lkb.doc) and saving the document either on a disk or on the computer's desktop.

Chapter Six

1. Here I refer to the substantial revision of the Online Writing Center that took place in 2001; I was not involved in the shaping or directing of previous versions of the Online Writing Center that functioned from 1997 to 2000.

2. The first Online Writing Center was created by Paul Brady and Billie Wahlstrom at the University of Minnesota, 1997. I was involved in a significant revision of the site in 2001.

3. WAC has also been referred to as "writing-in-the-disciplines" (WID) and "writing-intensive" (WI) movements. All labels refer to the integration of writing in all disciplinary instruction.

4. This was probably a reflection of the inadequacy of WebBoard technology at that time, for it tended to crash often and worked very slowly. Had the technology worked better, students may have used it more often.

Works Cited

Bakhtin, Mikhail. "The Problem of Speech Genres." *Speech Genres and Other Late Essays*. M. M. Bakhtin. Trans. Vern W. McGee. Austin, 1986. Reprinted by permission of the University of Texas Press, in *The Rhetorical Tradition: Readings from Classical Times to the Present*. Ed. Patricia Bizzell and Bruce Herzberg. Boston: Bedford-St. Martin's, 1990. 944–63. Page numbers cited in the text are to the reprint edition.

Barker, Thomas T., and Fred O. Kemp. "Network Theory: A Postmodern Pedagogy for the Writing Classroom." *Computers and Community: Teaching Composition in the Twenty-First Century*. Ed. Carolyn Handa. Portsmouth, NH: Boynton, 1990. 1–27.

Beebe, Randall L., and Mary J. Bonevelle. "The Culture of Technology in the Writing Center: Reinvigorating the Theory-Practice Debate." *Taking Flight with OWLs: Examining Electronic Writing Center Work*. Ed. James A. Inman and Donna N. Sewell. Mahwah, NJ: Lawrence Erlbaum Associates, 2000. 41–54.

Berge, Zane, and Mauri Collins, eds. *Computer Mediated Communication and the Online Classroom*. Cresskill, NJ: Hampton, 1995.

Bizzell, Patricia, and Bruce Herzberg. "Jacques Derrida." *The Rhetorical Tradition: Readings from Classical Times to the Present*. Ed. Patricia Bizzell and Bruce Herzberg. Boston: Bedford-St. Martin's, 1990. 1165–68.

Black, Laurel Johnson. *Between Talk and Teaching: Reconsidering the Writing Conference*. Logan: Utah State UP, 1998.

Bolter, Jay David. *Writing Space: The Computer, Hypertext, and the History of Writing*. Hillsdale, NJ: Lawrence Erlbaum Associates, 1991.

Bolter, Jay David, and Richard Grusin. *Remediation: Understanding New Media*. Cambridge, MA: MIT Press, 1999.

Bonk, Curtis Jay, and Donald J. Cunningham. "Searching for Learner-Centered, Constructivist, and Sociocultural Components of Collaborative Educational Learning Tools." *Electronic Collaborators: Learner-Centered Technologies for Literacy, Apprenticeship, and Discourse*. Ed. Curtis Jay Bonk and Kira S. King. Mahwah, NJ: Lawrence Erlbaum Associates, 1998. 25–50.

Bonk, Curtis Jay, and Kira S. King, eds. *Electronic Collaborators: Learner-Centered Technologies for Literacy, Apprenticeship, and Discourse*. Mahwah, NJ: Lawrence Erlbaum Associates, 1998.

Bowen, Betsy A. "Composition, Collaborations, and Computer-Mediated Conferencing." *The Online Writing Classroom.* Ed. Susanmarie Harrington, Rebecca Rickly, and Michael Day. Cresskill, NJ: Hampton, 2000. 129–46.

Brandt, Deborah. *Literacy as Involvement: The Acts of Writers, Readers, and Texts.* Carbondale: Southern Illinois UP, 1990.

Breuch, Lee-Ann M. Kastman, and Sam J. Racine. "Tutor Time Commitment in Online Writing Centers." *The Writing Lab Newsletter* 26.9 (2002): 10–13.

Bridwell, Lillian S. "Revising Strategies in Twelfth Grade Students' Transactional Writing." *Research in the Teaching of English* 14.3 (1980): 197–222.

Bridwell, Lillian S., and Donald Ross. "Integrating Computers into a Writing Curriculum; or, Buying, Begging, and Building." *The Computer in Composition Instruction: A Writer's Tool.* Ed. William Wresch. Urbana, IL: NCTE, 1984. 107–19.

Britton, James. "The Composing Processes and the Functions of Writing." *Research on Composing: Points of Departure.* Ed. Charles R. Cooper and Lee Odell. Urbana, IL: NCTE, 1978. 13–28.

Bruffee, Kenneth A. "Collaboration and the 'Conversation of Mankind.'" *College English* 46 (1984): 635–52.

——— . "Peer Tutoring and the 'Conversation of Mankind.'" *Writing Centers: Theory and Administration.* Ed. Gary A. Olson. Urbana, Ill: NCTE, 1984. 3–15.

——— . *Collaborative Learning: Higher Education, Interdependence, and the Authority of Knowledge.* 2nd ed. London: Johns Hopkins UP, 1999.

——— . *A Short Course in Writing.* 2nd ed. Boston: Little, 1990.

Burnett, Rebecca E. "Decision-Making during the Collaborative Planning of Coauthors." *Hearing Ourselves Think: Cognitive Research in the College Writing Classroom.* Ed. Ann M. Penrose and Barbara M. Sitko. New York: Oxford UP, 1993. 125–46.

——— . "Interactions of Engaged Supporters." *Making Thinking Visible: Writing, Collaborative Planning, and Classroom Inquiry.* Ed. Linda Flower, David L. Wallace, Linda Norris, and Rebecca E. Burnett. Urbana, IL: NCTE, 1994. 67–84.

——— . *Technical Communication.* 5th ed. New York: Harcourt, 2001.

Burnett, Rebecca E., and David Clark. "Shaping Technologies: The Complexity of Electronic Collaborative Interaction." *Computers and Technical Communication: Pedagogical and Programmatic Perspectives.* Ed. Stuart Selber. London: Ablex, 1997. 171–200.

Burnett, Rebecca E., and Lee-Ann Marie Kastman. "Teaching Composition: Current Theories and Practices." *Handbook of Academic Learning: Construction of Knowledge.* Ed. Gary D. Phye. New York: Academic, 1997. 268–301.

Castner, Joanna. "The Asynchronous, Online Writing Session: A Two-Way Stab in the Dark?" *Taking Flight with OWLs: Examining Electronic Writing Center Work.* Ed. James A. Inman and Donna N. Sewell. Mahwah, NJ: Lawrence Erlbaum Associates, 2000. 119–28.

Chapman, Orville, and Michael Fiore. "White Paper: A Description of CPR" (2001). 8 May 2002. <http://cpr.molsci.ucla.edu>.

Churchill, Elizabeth F., David N. Snowdon, and Alan J. Munro, eds. *Collaborative Virtual Environments: Digital Places and Spaces for Interaction.* London: Springer, 2001.

Clark, Beverly Lyon. *Talking about Writing: A Guide for Tutor and Teacher Conferences.* Ann Arbor: U of Michigan P, 1985.

Clark, Gregory. *Dialogue, Dialectic, and Conversation: A Social Perspective on the Function of Writing.* Carbondale: Southern Illinois UP, 1990.

Colativo, J. Rocky. "The Bytes Are On, But Nobody's Home: Composition's Wrong Turns into the Computer Age." *Reforming College Composition: Writing the Wrongs.* Ed. Ray Wallace, Alan Jackson, and Susan Lewis Wallace. London: Greenwood, 2000. 149–60.

Condon, William. "Virtual Space, Real Participation: Dimensions and Dynamics of a Virtual Classroom." *The Online Writing Classroom.* Ed. Susanmarie Harrington, Rebecca Rickly, and Michael Day. Cresskill, NJ: Hampton, 2000. 45–62.

Coogan, David. "Email 'Tutoring' as Collaborative Writing." *Wiring the Writing Center.* Ed. Eric H. Hobsen. Logan: Utah State UP, 1998. 25–43.

———. "The Idea of an Electronic Writing Center." Paper presented at the convention of the Conference on College Composition and Communication, Washington, D.C., March 1995.

Cooper, Marilyn M., and Cynthia L. Selfe. "Computer Conferences and Learning: Authority, Resistance, and Internally Persuasive Discourse." *College English* 52.8 (1990): 847–69.

Crafton, Robert E. "Promises, Promises: Computer-Assisted Revision and Basic Writers." *Computers and Composition* 13 (1996): 317–26.

Crump, Eric. "At Home in the MUD: Writing Centers Learn to Wallow." *High Wired: On the Design, Use, and Theory of Educational MOOs.* Ed. Cynthia Haynes and Jan Rune Holmevik. Ann Arbor: U of Michigan P, 1998. 177–91.

Cyganowski, Carol Klimick. "The Computer Classroom and Collaborative Learning: The Impact on Student Writers." *Computers and Community: Teaching Composition in the Twenty-First Century.* Ed. Carolyn Handa. Portsmouth, NH: Boynton-Heinemann, 1990. 68–88.

Dautermann, Jennie. "Writing with Electronic Tools in Midwestern Businesses." *Electronic Literacies in the Workplace: Technologies of Writing.* Ed. Patricia Sullivan and Jennie Dautermann. Urbana, IL: NCTE, 1996. 3–22.

Dautermann, Jennie, and Patricia Sullivan. "Introduction: Issues of Written Literacy and Electronic Literacy in Workplace Settings." *Electronic Literacies in the Workplace: Technologies of Writing*. Ed. Patricia Sullivan and Jennie Dautermann. Urbana, IL: NCTE, 1996. vii–xxxiii.

Dillenbourg, Pierre. "Introduction: What Do You Mean by 'Collaborative Learning'?" *Collaborative Learning: Cognitive and Computational Approaches*. Ed. Pierre Dillenbourg. New York: Pergamon, 1999. 1–19.

DiPardo, Anne, and Sarah Warshauer Freedman. "Peer Response Groups in the Writing Classroom: Theoretic Foundations and New Directions." *Review of Educational Research* 58.2 (1988): 119–49.

Dugger, William. "Standards for Technological Literacy." *Phi Delta Kappan* 82.7 (2001): 513–17.

Duin, Ann Hill, and Kathleen S. Gorak. *Writing with the Macintosh: Using Microsoft Word*. Cambridge, MA: Course Technology, 1991.

Duin, Ann Hill, and Craig Hansen. "Reading and Writing on Computer Networks as Social Construction and Social Interaction." *Literacy and Computers: The Complications of Teaching and Learning with Technology*. Ed. Cynthia L. Selfe and Susan Hilligoss. New York: MLA, 1994. 89–112.

Dumas, Joseph S., and Janice C. Redish. *A Practical Guide to Usability Testing*. Norwood, NJ: Ablex, 1993.

Elbow, Peter. *Writing without Teachers*. London: Oxford UP, 1973.

Emig, Janet. *The Composing Processes of Twelfth Graders*. Urbana, IL: NCTE, 1971.

Ewald, Helen Rothschild. "A Tangled Web of Discourses: On Post-Process Pedagogy and Communicative Interaction." *Post-Process Theory: Beyond the Writing-Process Paradigm*. Ed. Thomas Kent. Carbondale: Southern Illinois UP, 1999. 116–31.

Farkas, David K., and Steven E. Poltrock. "Online Editing, Mark-up Models, and the Workplace Lives of Editors and Writers." *Electronic Literacies in the Workplace: Technologies of Writing*. Ed. Patricia Sullivan and Jennie Dautermann. Urbana, IL: NCTE, 1996. 154–76.

Flores, Mary J. "Computer Conferencing: Composing a Feminist Community of Writers." *Computers and Community: Teaching Composition in the Twenty-First Century*. Ed. Carolyn Handa. Portsmouth, NH: Boynton, 1990. 106–17.

Flower, Linda, and John R. Hayes. "A Cognitive Process Theory of Writing." *College Composition and Communication* 32 (1981): 365–87.

——— . "Identifying the Organization of the Writing Processes." *Cognitive Processes in Writing*. Ed. Lee W. Gregg and Erwin R. Steinberg. Hillsdale, NJ: Lawrence Erlbaum Associates, 1980. 9–10.

Flower, Linda, David L. Wallace, Linda Norris, and Rebecca E. Burnett, eds. *Making Thinking Visible: Writing, Collaborative Planning, and Classroom Inquiry.* Urbana, IL: NCTE, 1994.

Forman, Janis. "Literacy, Collaboration, and Technology: New Connections and Challenges." *Literacy and Computers: The Complications of Teaching and Learning with Technology.* Ed. Cynthia L. Selfe and Susan Hilligoss. New York: MLA, 1994. 130–43.

Freedman, Sarah Warshauer, and Anne Marie Katz. "Pedagogical Interaction during the Composing Process: The Writing Conference." *Writing in Real Time: Modelling Production Processes.* Ed. Ann Matsuhashi. Norwood, NJ: Ablex, 1987. 58–80.

Galin, Jeffrey, and Joan Latchaw, eds. *The Dialogic Classroom: Teachers Integrating Computer Technology, Pedagogy, and Research.* Urbana, IL: NCTE, 1998.

———. "Voices That Let Us Hear: The Tale of the Borges Quest." *The Dialogic Classroom: Teachers Integrating Computer Technology, Pedagogy, and Research.* Ed. Jeffrey Galin and Joan Latchaw. Urbana, IL: NCTE, 1998. 43–66.

Gere, Anne Ruggles. *Writing Groups: History, Theory, and Implications.* Carbondale: Southern Illinois UP, 1987.

Gere, Anne Ruggles, and Robert D. Abbott. "Talking about Writing: The Language of Writing Groups." *Research in the Teaching of English* 19.4 (1985): 362–81.

Gere, Anne Ruggles and Ralph S. Stevens. "Writing Language Acquisition: The Role of Response and the Writing Conference." *The Acquisition of Written Language: Response and Revision.* Ed. Sarah Warshauer Freedman. Norwood, NJ: Ablex, 1985. 106–32.

Gross, Alan. *The Rhetoric of Science.* Cambridge: Harvard UP, 1990.

Gurak, Laura J. *Cyberliteracy: Navigating the Internet with Awareness.* London: Yale UP, 2001.

———. *Persuasion and Privacy in Cyberspace: The Online Protests over Lotus Marketplace and the Clipper Chip.* London: Yale UP, 1997.

Haas, Christina. *Writing Technology: Studies on the Materiality of Literacy.* Mahwah, NJ: Lawrence Erlbaum Associates, 1996.

Hackos, JoAnn T., and Janice C. Redish. *User and Task Analysis for Interface Design.* New York: Wiley Computer, 1998.

Hairston, Maxine. "The Winds of Change: Thomas Kuhn and the Revolution in the Teaching of Writing." *College Composition and Communication* 33.1 (February 1982): 76–88.

Halasek, Kay. *A Pedagogy of Possibility: Bakhtinian Perspectives on Composition Studies.* Carbondale: Southern Illinois UP, 1999.

Handa, Carolyn, ed. *Computers and Community: Teaching Composition in the Twenty-First Century.* Portsmouth, NH: Boynton, 1990.

Hansen, Craig. "Contextualizing Technology and Communication in a Corporate Setting." *Nonacademic Writing: Social Theory and Technology.* Ed. Ann Hill Duin and Craig Hansen. Mahwah: NJ: Lawrence Erlbaum Associates, 1996. 305–24.

Harrington, Susanmarie, Rebecca Rickly, and Michael Day, eds. *The Online Writing Classroom.* Cresskill, NJ: Hampton, 2000.

Harris, Muriel. "Collaboration Is Not Collaboration Is Not Collaboration: Writing Center Tutorials vs. Peer-Response Groups." *College Composition and Communication* 43.3 (1992): 369–83.

———. "Talking in the Middle: Why Writers Need Writing Tutors." *College English* 57.1 (1995): 27–42.

———. *Teaching One-to-One: The Writing Conference.* Urbana, IL: NCTE, 1986. 55–75.

———. "Using Computers to Expand the Role of Writing Centers." *Electronic Communication across the Curriculum.* Ed. Donna Reiss, Art Young, and Dickie Selfe. Urbana, IL: NCTE, 1998. 3–16.

Harris, Muriel, and Michael Pemberton. "Online Writing Labs (OWLs): A Taxonomy of Options and Issues." *Computers and Composition* 12.2 (1995): 145–59.

Hartman, Karen, Christine M. Neuwirth, Sara Kiesler, Lee Sproull, Cynthia Cochran, Michael Palmquist, and David Zubrow. "Patterns of Social Interaction and Learning to Write: Some Effects of Network Technologies." *Written Communication* 8.1 (1991): 79–113.

Hawisher, Gail E. "Blinding Insights: Classification Schemes and Software for Literacy Instruction." *Literacy and Computers: The Complications of Teaching and Learning with Technology.* Ed. Cynthia L. Selfe and Susan Hilligoss. New York: MLA, 1994. 37–55.

———. "The Effects of Word Processing on the Revision Strategies of College Freshmen." *Research in the Teaching of English* 21.2 (1987): 145–59.

Hawisher, Gail E., Paul LeBlanc, Charles Moran, and Cynthia L. Selfe. *Computers and the Teaching of Writing in American Higher Education, 1979–1994: A History.* Norwood, NJ: Ablex, 1996.

Hawkins, Thom. *Group Inquiry Techniques for Teaching Writing.* Urbana, IL: NCTE, 1976.

Henderson, Powell G. "Writing Technologies at White Sands." *Electronic Literacies in the Workplace: Technologies of Writing.* Ed. Patricia Sullivan and Jennie Dautermann. Urbana, IL: NCTE, 1996. 65–88.

Herrington, Anne. "Writing in Academic Settings: A Study of the Contexts for Writing in Two College Chemical Engineering Courses." *Research in the Teaching of English* 19 (1985): 331–61.

Hewett, Beth L. "Characteristics of Interactive Oral and Computer-mediated Peer Group Talk and Its Influence on Revision." *Computers and Composition* 17.3 (December 2000): 265–88.

Hiltz, Starr Roxanne, and Murray Turoff. *The Network Nation: Human Communication via Computer.* London: Addison-Wesley, 1978.

Hobsen, Eric H. "Straddling the Virtual Fence." *Wiring the Writing Center.* Ed. Eric H. Hobsen. Logan: Utah State UP, 1998. ix–xxvi.

———, ed. *Wiring the Writing Center.* Logan: Utah State UP, 1998.

Inman, James A. and Donna N. Sewell, eds. *Taking Flight with OWLs: Examining Electronic Writing Center Work.* Mahwah, NJ: Lawrence Erlbaum Associates, 2000.

Johnson, David W., Roger T. Johnson, and Karl A. Smith. *Active Learning: Cooperation in the College Classroom.* Edina, MN: Interaction, 1991.

Jordan-Henley, Jennifer, and Barry M. Maid. "Tutoring in Cyberspace: Student Impact and College/University Collaboration." *Computers and Composition* 12.2 (1998): 211–18.

Kang, Inae. "The Use of Computer-Mediated Communication: Electronic Collaboration and Interactivity." *Electronic Collaborators: Learner-Centered Technologies for Literacy, Apprenticeship, and Discourse.* Ed. Curtis Jay Bonk and Kira S. King. Mahwah, NJ: Lawrence Erlbaum Associates, 1998. 315–38.

Katz, Susan M. *The Dynamics of Writing Review: Opportunities for Growth and Change in the Workplace.* London: Ablex, 1998.

Kaufer, David S., and Kathleen M. Carley. *Communication at a Distance: The Influence of Print on Sociocultural Organization and Change.* Hillsdale, NJ: Lawrence Erlbaum Associates, 1993.

Kemp, Fred. "Surviving in English Departments: The Stealth Computer-Based Writing Program." *The Online Writing Classroom.* Ed. Susanmarie Harrington, Rebecca Rickly, and Michael Day. Cresskill, NJ: Hampton, 2000. 267–84.

Kent, Thomas, ed. *Post-Process Theory: Beyond the Writing Process Paradigm.* Carbondale: Southern Illinois UP, 1999.

Kiefer, Kathleen, and Charles R. Smith. "Improving Students' Revising and Editing: The Writer's Workbench System." *The Computer in Composition Instruction: A Writer's Tool.* Ed. William Wresch. Urbana, IL: NCTE, 1984. 65–82.

Kraemer, Kristi. "Revising Responding." *Peer Response Groups in Action: Writing Together in Secondary Schools.* Ed. Karen Spear. Portsmouth, NH: Boynton-Heinemann, 1993. 133–50.

Kuhn, Thomas S. *The Structure of Scientific Revolutions.* 3rd ed. Chicago: U of Chicago P, 1996.

Laney, Rebecca. "Letting Go." *Peer Response Groups in Action: Writing Together in Secondary Schools*. Ed. Karen Spear. Portsmouth, NH: Boynton-Heinemann, 1993. 151–61.

Langsam, Deborah M., and Kathleen Blake Yancey. "E-mailing Biology: Facing the Biochallenge." *Electronic Communication across the Curriculum*. Ed. Donna Reiss, Dickie Selfe, and Art Young. Urbana, IL: NCTE, 1998. 231–41.

Langston, M. Diane, and Trent W. Batson. "The Social Shifts Invited by Working Collaboratively on Computer Networks: The ENFI Project." *Computers and Community: Teaching Composition in the Twenty-First Century*. Ed. Carolyn Handa. Portsmouth, NH: Boynton, 1990. 140–59.

Lasarenko, Jane. "PR(OWL)ING AROUND: An OWL by Any Other Name." *Kairos: A Journal for Teachers of Writing in Webbed Environments* 1.1 (1996). 20 July 2002. <http://www.english.ttu.edu/Kairos/1.1/owls/lasarenko/prowl.html>.

Lea, Martin, and Russell Spears. "Computer-Mediated Communication, De-Individuation and Group Decision-Making." *International Journal of Man-Machine Studies* 34 (1991): 283–301.

———. "Paralanguage and Social Perception in Computer-Mediated Communication." *Journal of Organizational Computing* 2 (1992): 321–41.

LeBlanc, Paul J. "The Politics of Literacy and Technology in Secondary School Classrooms." *Literacy and Computers: The Complications of Teaching and Learning with Technology*. Ed. Cynthia L. Selfe and Susan Hilligoss. New York: MLA, 1994. 22–36.

LeFevre, Karen Burke. *Invention as a Social Act*. Carbondale: Southern Illinois UP, 1987.

Lunsford, Andrea. "Collaboration, Control, and the Idea of a Writing Center." *Writing Center Journal* 12.1 (1991): 3–10.

Mabrito, Mark. "Electronic Mail as a Vehicle for Peer Response." *Written Communication* 8.4 (October 1991): 509–32.

———. "E-mail Tutoring and Apprehensive Writers: What Research Tells Us." *Taking Flight with OWLs: Examining Electronic Writing Center Work*. Ed. James A. Inman and Donna N. Sewell. Mahwah, NJ: Lawrence Erlbaum Associates, 2000. 141–50.

MacKenzie, Colleen. "The Need for a Design Lexicon: Examining Minimalist, Performance-centered, and User-centered Design." *Technical Communication* 49.4 (2002): 405–10.

Marcus, Stephen. "Real-Time Gadgets with Feedback: Special Effects in Computer-Assisted Writing." *The Computer in Composition Instruction: A Writer's Tool*. Ed. William Wresch. Urbana, IL: NCTE, 1984. 120–30.

Martindale, Michael J. "Mental Models and Text Schemas: Why Computer Based Tutorials Should Be Considered a Communication Medium." *Journal of Computer-Based Instruction* 20.4 (1993): 107–12.

Mehlenbacher, Brad. "Technologies and Tensions: Designing Online Environments for Teaching Technical Communication." *Computers and Technical Communication: Pedagogical and Programmatic Perspectives*. Ed. Stuart Selber. London: Ablex, 1997. 201–18.

Meyer, Emily, and Louise Z. Smith. *The Practical Tutor*. New York: Oxford UP, 1987.

Mirel, Barbara. "Writing and Database Technology: Extending the Definition of Writing in the Workplace." *Electronic Literacies in the Workplace: Technologies of Writing*. Ed. Patricia Sullivan and Jennie Dautermann. Urbana, IL: NCTE, 1996. 91–114.

Monroe, Barbara. "The Look and Feel of the OWL Conference." *Wiring the Writing Center*. Ed. Eric Hobsen. Logan: Utah State UP, 1998. 3–24.

Murphy, Christina, and Steve Sherwood. "The Tutoring Process: Exploring Paradigms and Practices." *The St. Martin's Sourcebook for Writing Tutors*. Ed. Christina Murphy and Steve Sherwood. New York: St. Martin's, 1995. 1–18.

Murray, Donald. *A Writer Teaches Writing: A Practical Method of Teaching Composition*. Boston: Houghton, 1968.

Myers, Greg. *Writing Biology: Texts in the Social Construction of Scientific Knowledge*. Madison: U of Wisconsin P, 1990.

Myers-Breslin, Linda. "Technology, Distance, and Collaboration: Where Are These Pedagogies Taking Composition?" *Reforming College Composition: Writing the Wrongs*. Ed. Ray Wallace, Alan Jackson, and Susan Lewis Wallace. London: Greenwood, 2000. 161–78.

Newkirk, Thomas. "Direction and Misdirection in Peer Response." *College Composition and Communication* 35.3 (1984): 301–11.

Nielsen, Jakob. *Usability Engineering*. San Diego, CA: Academic, 1993.

North, Stephen. "The Idea of a Writing Center." *College English* 46.4 (1984): 433–46.

Olson, Gary A., ed. *Writing Centers: Theory and Administration*. Urbana, IL: NCTE, 1984.

Ong, Walter J. *Orality and Literacy: The Technologizing of the Word*. London: Routledge, 1982.

Palloff, Rena M., and Keith Pratt. *Lessons from the Cyberspace Classroom: The Realities of Online Teaching*. San Francisco: Jossey, 2001.

Palmquist, Michael E. "Network-Supported Interaction in Two Writing Classrooms." *Computers and Composition* 9.4 (1993): 25–57.

Palmquist, Michael, Kate Kiefer, James Hartvigsen, and Barbara Goodlew. *Transitions: Teaching Writing in Computer-Supported and Traditional Classrooms.* London: Ablex, 1997.

Palmquist, Michael, and Donald E. Zimmerman. *Writing with a Computer.* Needham Heights, MA: Allyn, 1999.

Peckham, Irvin. "If It Ain't Broke, Why Fix It? Disruptive and Constructive Computer-Mediated Response Group Practices." *Computers and Composition* 13.3 (1996): 327–39.

Plato. *Phaedrus.* Trans. H. N. Fowler. Reprinted with permission in *The Rhetorical Tradition: Readings from Classical Times to the Present.* Ed. Patricia Bizzell and Bruce Herzberg. Boston: Bedford-St. Martin's, 1990. 113–43.

Powers, Judith K., and Jane V. Nelson. "Rethinking Writing Center Conferencing Strategies for Writers in the Disciplines." *The Writing Lab Newsletter* 20.1 (1995): 12–16.

Price, Jonathan. *Outlining Goes Electronic.* Stamford, CT: Ablex, 1999.

"Professional Counseling Journals: Implementing On-Line Editing and Peer Review." Editorial. *Counselor Education and Supervision* 40 (2000): 2–7.

Redish, Janice C. "What Is Information Design?" *Technical Communication* 47.2 (2000): 163–68.

Reed, W. Michael. "The Effects of Computer-Based Writing Instruction and Mode of Discourse on Writing Performance and Writer Anxieties." *Computers in Human Behavior* 6 (1990): 211–21.

Reigstad, Thomas J., and Donald A. McAndrew. *Training Tutors for Writing Conferences.* Urbana, IL: NCTE, 1984.

Reiss, Donna, Dickie Selfe, and Art Young, eds. *Electronic Communication across the Curriculum.* Urbana, IL: NCTE, 1998.

Rickly, Rebecca. "Reflection and Responsibility in (Cyber) Tutor Training: Seeing Ourselves Clearly on and off the Screen." *Wiring the Writing Center.* Ed. Eric H. Hobsen. Logan: Utah State UP, 1998. 44–61.

Rorty, Richard. *Contingency, Irony, and Solidarity.* New York: Cambridge UP, 1989.

———. "Inquiry as Recontextualization: An Anti-Dualist Account of Interpretation." *The Interpretive Turn.* Ed. David R. Hiley, James F. Bohman, and Richard Shusterman. Ithaca: Cornell UP, 1991. 59–80.

———. *Philosophy and the Mirror of Nature.* Princeton: Princeton UP, 1979.

Rubin, Jeffrey. *Handbook of Usability Testing: How to Plan, Design, and Conduct Effective Tests.* New York: Wiley, 1994.

Rushton, Christopher, Phillip Ramsey, and Roy Rada. "Peer Assessment in a Collaborative Hypermedia Environment: A Case Study." *Journal of Computer-Based Instruction* 20.3 (1993): 75–80.

Russell, David. "Activity Theory and Process Approaches: Writing (Power) in School and Society." *Post-Process Theory: Beyond the Writing-Process Paradigm.* Ed. Thomas Kent. Carbondale: Southern Illinois UP, 1999. 80–95.

Russell, David R. *Writing in the Academic Disciplines, 1870–1990: A Curricular History.* Carbondale: Southern Illinois UP, 1991.

Russell, Scott. "Clients Who Frequent Madam Barnett's Emporium." *The Writing Center Journal* 20.1 (1999): 61–72.

Russell, Thomas. "Technology Wars: Winners and Losers." *Educom Review* 32.2 (14 November 1998). 21 August 2002. <http://www.educause.edu/pub/er/review/reviewArticles/32244.html>.

Selber, Stuart A. "Introduction." *Computers and Technical Communication: Pedagogical and Programmatic Perspectives.* Ed. Stuart Selber. London: Ablex, 1997. 1–16.

Selfe, Cynthia L. *Creating a Computer-Supported Writing Facility: A Blueprint for Action.* Houghton, MI: Computers and Composition, 1989.

———. *Technology and Literacy in the Twenty-First Century.* Carbondale: Southern Illinois UP, 1999.

———. "Technology in the English Classroom: Computers through the Lens of Feminist Theory." *Computers and Community: Teaching Composition in the Twenty-First Century.* Ed. Carolyn Handa. Portsmouth, NH: Boynton, 1990. 118–39.

Shadle, Mark. "The Spotted OWL: Online Writing Labs as Sites of Diversity, Controversy, and Identity." *Taking Flight with OWLs: Examining Electronic Writing Center Work.* Ed. James A. Inman and Donna N. Sewell. Mahwah, NJ: Lawrence Erlbaum Associates, 2000. 3–16.

Shamoon, Linda K., and Deborah H. Burns. "A Critique of Pure Tutoring." *The Writing Center Journal* 15.2 (Spring 1995): 134–51.

Sims, Brenda R. "Electronic Mail in Two Corporate Workplaces." *Electronic Literacies in the Workplace: Technologies of Writing.* Ed. Patricia Sullivan and Jennie Dautermann. Urbana, IL: NCTE, 1996. 41–64.

Sirc, Geoffrey, and Tom Reynolds. "The Face of Collaboration in the Networked Writing Classroom." *Computers and Composition* 7 (1990): 53–70.

Skubikowski, Kathleen, and John Elder. "Computers and the Social Contexts of Writing." *Computers and Community: Teaching Composition in the Twenty-First Century.* Ed. Carolyn Handa. Portsmouth, NH: Boynton, 1990. 89–105.

Sommers, Nancy. "Responding to Student Writing." *College Composition and Communication* 33.2 (1982): 148–56.

———. "Revision Strategies of Student Writers and Experienced Adult Writers." *College Composition and Communication* 31 (1980): 378–88.

Spear, Karen, ed. *Peer Response Groups in Action: Writing Together in Secondary Schools.* Portsmouth, NH: Heinemann, 1993.

———. *Sharing Writing: Peer Response Groups in English Classes.* Portsmouth, NH: Boynton-Heinemann, 1988.

Sperling, Melanie. "Dialogues of Deliberation: Conversation in the Teacher-Student Writing Conference." *Written Communication* 8.2 (1991): 131–62.

———. "I Want to Talk to Each of You: Collaboration and the Teacher-Student Writing Conference." *Research in the Teaching of English* 24.3 (1990): 279–321.

Sperling, Melanie, and Sarah Warshauer Freedman. "A Good Girl Writes Like a Good Girl: Written Response to Student Writing." *Written Communication* 4.4 (1987): 343–69.

Spigelman, Candace. *Across Property Lines: Textual Ownership in Writing Groups.* Carbondale: Southern Illinois UP, 2000.

Spinuzzi, Clay. "Designing for Lifeworlds: Genre and Activity in Information Systems Design and Evaluation." Diss., Iowa State University, 1999.

Spool, Jared, Tara Scanlan, Bill Schroeder, Carolyn Snyder, and Terri DeAngelo. *Web Site Usability: A Designer's Guide.* <http://www.uie.com/bookdesc.htm>.

Straub, Richard. *The Practice of Response: Strategies for Commenting on Student Writing.* Cresskill, NJ: Hampton, 2000.

Tornow, Joan. *Link/Age: Composing in the Online Classroom.* Logan: Utah State UP, 1997.

Tyner, Kathleen. *Literacy in a Digital World: Teaching and Learning in the Age of Information.* Mahwah, NJ: Lawrence Erlbaum Associates, 1998.

Virzi, Robert. "Refining the Test Phase of Usability Evaluation: How Many Subjects Is Enough?" *Human Factors* 34 (1992): 457–68.

Vygotsky, Lev. *Thought and Language.* London: MIT P, 1986.

Wahlstrom, Billie J. "Communication and Technology: Defining a Feminist Presence in Research and Practice." *Literacy and Computers: The Complications of Teaching and Learning with Technology.* Ed. Cynthia L. Selfe and Susan Hilligoss. New York: MLA, 1994. 171–85.

———. "Teaching and Learning Communities: Locating Literacy, Agency, and Authority in a Digital Domain." *Computers and Technical Communication: Pedagogical and Programmatic Perspectives.* Ed. Stuart Selber. London: Ablex, 1997. 129–48.

Wallace, David L. "Teaching Collaborative Planning: Creating a Social Context for Writing." *Making Thinking Visible: Writing, Collaborative Planning, and Classroom Inquiry.* Ed. Linda Flower, David L. Wallace, Linda Norris, and Rebecca E. Burnett. Urbana, IL: NCTE, 1994. 48–66.

Wallace, David L., and John R. Hayes. "Redefining Revision for Freshman." *Research in the Teaching of English* 25.1 (1991): 54–66.

Walther, Joseph B. "Computer-Mediated Communication: Impersonal, Interpersonal, and Hyperpersonal Interaction." *Communication Research* 23.1 (1996): 3–43.

Warshauer, Mark. *Electronic Literacies: Language, Culture, and Power in Online Education.* Mahwah, NJ: Lawrence Erlbaum Associates, 1999.

Wresch, William, ed. *The Computer in Composition Instruction: A Writer's Tool.* Urbana, IL: NCTE, 1984.

Young, Richard. "Paradigms and Problems: Needed Research in Rhetorical Invention." *Research on Composing: Points of Departure.* Ed. Charles R. Cooper and Lee Odell. Urbana, IL: NCTE, 1978. 29–48.

Zuboff, Shoshana. *In the Age of the Smart Machine: The Future of Work and Power.* New York: Basic, 1984.